PRAISE F(

# THE LOVE EVERYBODY WANTS

"In her new book, *The Love Everybody Wants,* Madison Prewett Troutt shares her heart for God-honoring relationships with passion and compassion. Packed with incredibly wise, practical insights and biblical truths, this book will help you find the love that lasts and transforms lives. Anyone seeking to deepen their understanding of love and build stronger relationships with those around them will appreciate this message."

—CRAIG AND AMY GROESCHEL, founding pastors of
Life.Church and authors of *From This Day Forward*

"Waiting to be loved can be one of the loneliest places in the world, which often leads us to compromise. I love that Madi shares the truths on why the right person is worth the wait and how God wants to use this season to lavish you with *his* love! Madison does not shy away from the hard topics and always brings it back to what God says about you."

—BRITTANY AND BRANDON LAKE, Grammy
Award–winning singer-songwriter

"*The Love Everybody Wants* is a much-needed breath of fresh air in our dating-crazed culture. Every page feels like you're sitting down having coffee with your best friend or favorite big sister, getting to hear how she navigated love, heartbreak, and everything in between. This book reminds us that true love is still possible and that God can turn the pain of our past into something more beautiful than we can imagine."

—EARL AND ONEKA MCCLELLAN,
pastors of Shoreline City Church

"This book will not only help you navigate singleness and relationships, but it will also help you love God more. Madi's journey to marriage is so relatable, entertaining, and inspiring! She will minister to you and your friends while giving you great relationship advice and helping you realize the love you already have."

—JONATHAN POKLUDA, lead pastor of Harris Creek
Baptist Church, bestselling author of *Outdated,*
and host of the podcast *Becoming Something*

"Reading this book was like having a sister eloquently express everything I've felt while looking for love in all the wrong places. It is a kind yet firm reminder that we are more valuable than we can possibly imagine."

—JESS AND BEN HIGGINS, author, podcast host,
and social media influencers

"Madi is fiercely in love with Jesus. Ultimately, there is no other love that will satisfy. But *The Love Everybody Wants* will be a helpful guide for all of it—loving God and wrestling with our desires for love on earth too. This book will give you hope!"

—JENNIE ALLEN, *New York Times* bestselling author

"As a dating coach who gets to work with hundreds of single Christian women, I find this book to be profound. Madi addresses so many lies believed by singles, as well as ways to conquer those lies and fight for truth and freedom. There are so many tools for healing and wisdom in these pages that every single Christian woman (at any age) needs to hear and be reminded of."

—KAIT TOMLIN, bestselling author, dating coach,
and founder of Heart of Dating

# THE
# LOVE
# EVERYBODY
# WANTS

# THE LOVE EVERYBODY WANTS

## What You're Looking For Is Already Yours

### MADISON PREWETT TROUTT

FOREWORD BY
**AUDREY ROLOFF**

WATERBROOK

Details in some anecdotes and stories have been changed to protect the identities of the persons involved.

2024 WaterBrook Trade Paperback Edition

Published in the United States by WaterBrook, an imprint of Random House, a division of Penguin Random House LLC.

WATERBROOK and colophon are registered trademarks of Penguin Random House LLC.

Originally published in hardcover and in slightly different form in the United States by WaterBrook, an imprint of Random House, a division of Penguin Random House LLC, in 2023.

Grateful acknowledgment is made to HarperCollins Christian Publishing for permission to reprint excerpts from *Made for This Moment* by Madison Prewett, copyright © 2021 by Madison Prewett. Used by permission of HarperCollins Christian Publishing, www.harpercollinschristian.com.

The Library of Congress catalog record is available at https://lccn.loc.gov/2023002287.

Printed in the United States of America on acid-free paper

waterbrookmultnomah.com

1st Printing

Book design by Jo Anne Metsch

Most WaterBrook books are available at special quantity discounts for bulk purchase for premiums, fundraising, and corporate and educational needs by organizations, churches, and businesses. Special books or book excerpts also can be created to fit specific needs. For details, contact specialmarketscms@penguinrandomhouse.com.

*This book is dedicated to my husband, Grant Michael Troutt. I am so proud to be yours, but I am even more proud of the man of God you are. Thank you for always pointing me back to the greatest love of all: Jesus. I love you forever!*

# FOREWORD

If you've picked up this book, my guess is that your heart desires a love that's characterized by all the "un's": *unquenchable, undivided, unconditional, unlimited, unending.* It's in our human nature to long for a love like this, but it's not in our human nature to live like we already have it. And the truth is, we do. You do. You are already loved by God more than you could ever possibly imagine, and there is nothing you can do to make him love you any more or less than he does right now. Even if you never love him back, he will keep loving and pursuing you. There really is no greater love than this.

Imagine you are in a dating relationship where you are so in love with your boyfriend and you are pursuing, encouraging, and desiring to love, serve, and respect him, but he never shows you any love in return. You'd probably dump him. And I'd hope that you would. Love runs weary when unreciprocated. But not God's love. He loves you better than any human ever could, with all the "un's," even if it's never reciprocated. There is a verse in the Bible (1 John 3:1) that says, "See what great love the Father has lavished on us, that we should be called children of God! And that is what we are!" That is what you are. A child of a God who lavishes his love on you so deeply and fully. So, you want that kind of deep, real, lasting, intimate, faithful, trustworthy, forever kind of love? As Madi so beautifully portrays in these pages, *what you are looking for is already yours.*

Back in 2020 I happened to watch an episode of Madi's season of *The Bachelor* with some friends and was immediately intrigued by Madi. There was a joy, peace, and confidence that she carried in a chaotic and, dare I say, unhealthy environment that set her apart. While all the girls seemed to be searching for love, it was evident that Madi *lived* loved. I could sense her love for God before she verbally expressed it because I share that same love. And when you know that love—God's love—you can't help but see it in other people.

As Madi's *Bachelor* relationship was publicly displayed on TV, I felt a nudge to reach out to her because I had also dated a boy in front of millions of viewers. For context, my husband grew up on reality television, so our dating relationship, our wedding day, and even the early years of our marriage were on public display to be both praised and ridiculed. The unconventional position I found myself in came with its own set of struggles that were unrelatable to my friends, which left me feeling isolated. My heart felt for Madi as I remembered that season of my life, so I reached out to her on social media and asked for her address, hoping to mail her a little encouragement. Thankfully she responded, so I sent her a little package of goodies.

A week or so later, I got a message from Madi saying that she was truly blessed to receive the goodies. Since then, it's been a joy to grow in friendship with Madi and to cheer her on as she boldly and gracefully shares truth to a generation so consumed by lies—something she does beautifully in the pages that follow.

If you've picked up this book in hopes of figuring out how to find the perfect spouse, this is not it. And, might I boldly add, there is no such book. But what I am so excited for you to discover in these pages is the practical wisdom for pursuing healthy relationships, the comfort of hearing difficult truths from someone who's been there, the deeper understanding that will come from asking the hard questions, and ultimately a deeper understanding of how infinitely loved you are by God.

In the words of Martina McBride, "This one's for the girls." And not just the girls who have ever had a broken heart or wished upon a shooting star or loved without holding back or dreamed with everything they have. This book is also for the girls who have felt the pressure to prove or perform to earn love. For the girls who have allowed shame, fear, guilt, doubt, or comparison to hold them back from experiencing true love. For the girls who are single and confused by the dating world and not sure what to even be looking for in a man of integrity. For the girls who are dating someone but aren't sure if it's the "forever" kind of someone. For the girls who want to start their marriage on a healthy foundation but don't have a healthy example of a loving relationship to learn from. And for the girls who desire a love story marked by the "un's."

As Madi says, there is a better way to approach our desire for love that is hardwired in our hearts. And it's this—that we must look to God first, learn to see ourselves as he sees us, and only then will we be ready to love whoever God brings into our lives. When you pursue a real relationship with God and allow him to fill you with the joy, peace, freedom, and love that only he can, *that* is living loved. And that love is infinite, and it's available to you now. As you read this book, I hope you see just how real, healing, transforming, and beautiful that love is—and that you not only see it but also experience it. *I hope you realize that what you are looking for is already yours.*

—AUDREY ROLOFF, *New York Times* bestselling co-author of *A Love Letter Life* and founder of *The Marriage Journal*

# CONTENTS

# THE
# LOVE
# EVERYBODY
# WANTS

# 1

## LOOKING FOR LOVE
### Searching in All the Right Places

We love *love*. We love the rush that bubbles up inside when we think about it. We can easily be swept up. Obsessed. Infatuated. We are hardwired for connection. We want to be seen, known, and, yes, loved. We want to be chosen, to be valued. Maybe you could even say we are made to love. But it doesn't take a PhD in the psychology of modern romance to know that finding deep love and connection is, well, not easy.

I know this has been true for me. Want a sneak peek of the real conversation going on in my head when I started to write this book as a single woman?

*How many more wrong ones until the right one?*
*Is there something wrong with me?*

*Do I settle for good enough?*

*What if no one else will love me?*

*What if I end up alone?*

*What if I get hurt again?*

*Why is it so hard to let go?*

*Am I hard to love?*

*Am I enough?*

*Ugh, why can't relationships be easy?*

*How many more breakups until I finally get the whole "till death do us part"?*

*How many more tears and fears until peace and joy?*

*Will I ever be happy?*

My guess is I'm not alone in constantly asking these questions. We're glued to our phones, social media, and TV dating shows. We're bombarded with images of love and relationships and sex and happiness and weddings and influencers who seem to have picture-perfect lives. But so many of us feel alone and confused. We're asking, *Why hasn't love panned out for me? I'm tired of not being chosen.*

It might come as a surprise to some that I struggle with this—but I do. You may know me from season 24 of ABC's *The Bachelor,* which aired in 2020. You may have read my first book, *Made for This Moment.* Or maybe you have no idea who I am, but you're desperately hoping to hear something refreshing and helpful on the topic of love. Something that goes beyond "Don't have sex until you're married" and "Wait on God's timing." Though I've tried to put both of those pieces of advice into practice myself, I know that something *more* is needed during the in-between. We need something greater than a list of rules so that if we do meet our someone, we're ready for them.

Trust me—I did plenty of dating "Madi's way" and ended up with regret. I wound up hurt and feeling either like I was being rejected or like I was wasting valuable time and emotions. I'm not perfect and will never claim to be—just ask my friends and family! But I *have* suffered to the point that I was willing to do something different in order to find peace and joy. I stopped searching for love and instead started at the foundation of love itself—by learning to bring my longings to God and to accept and love myself first.

By the way, I think it's worth mentioning that loving yourself doesn't always look how culture and social media make it look. It's not just about posting workout selfies or getting massages with girlfriends. More on that later, but another goal of this book is to encourage you to look beyond what you see online and on TV. Not just about love, but about people's lives. Those are such one-dimensional portrayals of reality. I should know—people are always shocked when they get to know me and see that I'm just as insecure, just as tired of dating, and just as worn out as they are. I *was* anyway. What happened in between the worn-out and where I am now?

That's exactly what I'm going to tell you.

But first let me say, there are no simple answers to questions on dating and marriage, mostly because our hearts are funny things, and people aren't always simple. A quick internet search reveals plenty of people eager to dish out oversimplified relationship advice. But here's what I want to tell you: I think there is a better way. A deeper way. A way forward that sets our hearts in order and helps us see our longings and experiences in a new light.

And before you think I'm setting out to write a "how to get a boyfriend" book, you should know that's not the goal. I want to show you how to look to God, see yourself, and find deep love amid our culture's shallow ideas about romance.

Because the truth is, finding the love everybody wants isn't nearly as complicated as we've made it. In fact, the Bible tells us pretty clearly how love works in Matthew 22:35–39—my inspiration for writing this book:

> One of them, an expert in the law, tested him with this question: "Teacher, which is the greatest commandment in the Law?"
>
> Jesus replied: "'Love the Lord your God with all your heart and with all your soul and with all your mind.' This is the first and greatest commandment. And the second is like it: 'Love your neighbor as yourself.'"

*"Love the Lord your God with all your heart and with all your soul and with all your mind." This is the first and greatest commandment. And the second is like it: "Love your neighbor as yourself."*

First and foremost, we must set our hearts right with God, know the depths of his love for us, and believe that his words about us are true. Then comes the often-difficult work of learning to love ourselves. When we get those two relationships where they should be, only then can we start to talk about loving other people, whether that's cultivating a deep community of friends, better relationships with family, or a romantic relationship—all three of which combine to create a healthy support system.

If you want to use a tried-and-true metaphor, imagine your life as a house. Your relationship with God is the foundation. Your relationship with yourself is the framework and walls. You can't start adding furniture and decorations before the foundation and walls are in place. I mean, you can try. But you won't be successful.

The message of this book isn't that the ultimate finish line in life is to find a spouse and live happily ever after or that in order to be happy or have purpose, you have to find your person. It's not my intention to help you get married off. My goal is for you to understand that while we aren't made to go through life alone, we can't expect to have thriving friendships or romantic relationships until we've established our relationships with God and with ourselves.

What if we *never* find the person we're searching for? Does that mean we can't be fulfilled? I remember being young and praying, "God, I trust you in everything, but I'm kind of hoping that singleness is not your will for my life." Why is that? Why do so many of us connect marriage with wholeness? The truth is that as I've grown older, I've experienced the ways building meaningful relationships with God and with ourselves leaves little room for loneliness or unfulfillment.

On the search for a deeper understanding of love, we all

must work through the clichés and shallow ideas we've come to accept as truth—ideas like, *If I just had a significant other, I would feel whole* and *I have to follow my heart above all else.* While there are obviously wonderful aspects of being with another person, these ideas aren't the fullest expression of God's love and calling for us. That's not to say we should ignore our emotions. That would be unrealistic—impossible, even. But we can't be controlled by our emotions either.

These clichés can make their way into our hearts and influence how we think things should be. We often think we're owed love the way the world defines it. In light of that, each of the following chapter titles is a common phrase related to dating and relationships that has become ingrained in our vocabulary through social media and culture. I want to help you examine these ideas and evaluate the truth of them. And in doing so, I believe we can arrive at a deeper understanding of what God says about love, because it's only by embracing this understanding that we can experience peace, joy, and wholeness without fear for our future.

In this book, I'll lay out some of the issues we're facing emotionally and spiritually, addressing everything from social media relationship trends to biblical insights into God's ideas for marriage and identity. Together, we'll tackle love, faith, dating culture, and personal worth in a refreshing manner. Beginning in chapter 2, you'll find QR codes embedded at the end of each chapter. These links will direct you to short videos and other digital resources covering a range of topics—things like the essentials I look for in a relationship, prayers for when your heart is hurting, and words for seasons of waiting. My prayer is that as I share my experience, you'll be encouraged no matter where you are in life.

> *We're made for love, but it takes work to get these loves in order.*

When we can learn to see relationships with God, ourselves, and others in whole, holy, and healthy ways, our hearts will stop looking for love in the wrong places. We're made for love, but it takes work to get these loves in order. But believe me when I say, it's possible to know the love of God. It's possible to love—and maybe even like—yourself. It's possible to navigate the matrix of relationships with confidence and hope. It's possible to look out to your future with joy—because you were made for love.

## PROOF OF PROMISE

When I started writing this book, I was single. Again.

But at some point during this publishing journey, I met someone. *My* someone. Grant. He came at the perfect time— God's time. You'll hear more about Grant as we walk through these chapters together.

I don't claim to have mastered my relationship with God or with myself, but I have learned a few invaluable lessons on the way. I've learned that those connections must be my priority. Not just while I'm single, but throughout my entire life. Not just because it's those connections that best prepare me to take on the title *wife*, but because that's how we're wired to live our most meaningful and joy-filled lives.

*Wife! What?!*

I know. I'm just as shocked as you are. But then again, I'm not.

We're all looking for the same kind of love. But my goal is to show you that the love everybody wants is already ours.

# 2

## HE LOVES ME, HE LOVES ME NOT
### Redefining True Love

*Is there something wrong with me?*
*Am I even worthy of true love?*
*Will I ever find the love everybody wants?*

These are questions I asked constantly growing up. By the time I was in my twenties, I'd had enough of love. I felt exhausted, hopeless, and angry. Why couldn't I get love right? Why were relationships so hard? Was I not worthy of the love everybody wants? I knew I was too young to feel so cynical toward relationships. It felt like I was drowning in a sea of self-doubt, with waves of self-imposed pressure. I would do anything for a breath of belonging or to feel enough, even if just for a moment.

What started as just thoughts then became my identity. I couldn't see anyone else's needs, because I was so consumed with meeting my own. I couldn't love others well, because I was so desperate to be loved. I couldn't serve others, because

I was constantly striving to prove I was worthy of being picked.

I knew that there had to be a better way. I started asking questions. I went to the Bible, I confided in mentors, and I did some soul-searching. Why did looking for love—something that seems to make other people feel so good—make me feel so *bad*?

In tracking down my sense of unworthiness, I looked back and saw sixteen-year-old Madi in a bathroom stall with her head buried in her hands, crying. She was overwhelmed with hurt. How could her first love reject her? In her mind, his cheating meant rejection and his rejection meant that she wasn't enough. She wasn't enough, because there was someone better and he picked *that other girl*. I then realized that young Madi's reaction was to develop an overachieving, performance-based mindset, doing everything she could to prove she should always be the first pick. From a place of fear and hurt, she built walls all around her broken and hurting heart.

After that moment in the bathroom stall, young Madi began to seek worth in getting attention from guys. Winning them over brought a rush of emotion, and as soon as she won them over, she would dump them because they no longer served a purpose. They proved she was worthy of their attention. They proved she was their first choice. This performance-based mindset trickled into everything. School, faith, family, friendships, and identity. Despite the momentary breaths of air that achievement gave her, the sea just continued to deepen.

Like any other unhealthy coping mechanism, getting attention from guys was a *very* temporary fix. Over time, I became restless. Though I wasn't sure then what the root issue was, I see now how I was longing for the type of love I couldn't get from a guy. I was longing for something *deep* and *fulfilling* that would last forever. In the meantime, I was hurting myself. But more than that, I was hurting other people. While this is certainly nothing to be proud of, it was reality.

Freshman year of college, I realized I needed to deal with the monster I had allowed to rob me of the confident, content, and purposeful life God had called me to live. After years of chasing the high of male attention, I was tired of being tired. I was tired of hurting, tired of hurting others, and tired of the way looking for love made me feel. Change happened not in an instant but over time, after a lot of trial and error. But in that moment of realization, I finally confronted the lies that were born in that tear-filled moment in the bathroom stall years earlier. I decided to deal with the fear and shame that followed. I looked in the eyes of my sixteen-year-old self, lifted my head, and simply said, "I am sorry for what he did to you. But don't let his inability to see your worth make you question it. You have nothing to prove. You are picked and you are loved."

It was a powerful moment—going back to where the lie was born. Going back to where the pains of rejection began. If you can do that—if you can remember the first time you felt unworthy, unvaluable, and rejected, I'd encourage you to name that experience for yourself.

Maybe it was a teacher, coach, or parent. Maybe it was a guy you liked or a boyfriend. Maybe it was a friend or group of people who wouldn't accept you. Whatever that first moment of rejection was for you, evaluating the validity of your feelings is a step toward healing. I think that's a great place for us to start together in this book.

Do you also feel like you're drowning? Maybe you've covered it up with makeup and tight clothes. With filters and Photoshop. You've put up walls of protection, promising yourself you will never feel that pain again. And somewhere along the way, you began to believe the lie that you're unworthy of love. But maybe the truth is that you're not bad at love; you've just been chasing the wrong definition of love. Maybe by redefining what true love is, we can finally embrace what's already ours and find the love we're meant for.

Ready to get started? To experience life change? To find the great love you were meant for? Then just like Shania Twain says, "Let's go, girls."[1]

*Maybe the truth is that you're not bad at love; you've just been chasing the wrong definition of love.*

## HE LOVES ME . . .

"He loves me, he loves me not . . ."

Did you ever play that game where you run outside, grab a flower, and rip the petals off one by one to figure out how your crush really feels about you? No? Just me? Cool.

Either way, you've probably been there, if not literally with a flower, then with life. Riding on the highs of "He loves me!" and suffering during the lows of "He loves me not."

My thoughts have bounced back and forth between these

lines of thinking more times than I can count. I picture that silly game and those flower petals falling and have come to realize that most of us still somehow believe the lie that *this* is what love is. That it's inconsistent. Unstable. Performance based. Uncertain. Immature. Emotional. A roller coaster. Sometimes causing us to lose ourselves or change ourselves, thinking, *If I look like _____, then I will be worthy of love.* Or, *If I give him what he wants, then maybe he will choose me.*

But then what happens when we change and compromise and settle . . . and we still don't feel like we're enough and we still don't feel loved?

Each petal that falls off leaves us feeling more unsure, unsafe, and pressured. We stay on edge. Depressed and suffering inside, battling the feelings of rejection and not being enough. We don't know what it's like to feel safe, peaceful, stable, and secure. Security is a foreign concept when we base our self-worth on the highs of other people's acceptance and the lows of our own underperformance.

I now wonder why we were so willing to look to chance and risk to determine our future—having our hope cling to the last flower petal or winning a bet over a silly game of rock, paper, scissors. Is it because these seem to be types of "hope" that we can bet on and "see"—in other words, because it's tangible? But that kind of fate isn't reliable or sustainable, or even real. It's a game.

So, what is love? Is it just a feeling? Is it attraction? Chemistry and passion? Is it rewards based—in other words, will a guy love you as long as you're who and what he wants you to be?

What if love wasn't built on other people's approval or acceptance? What if it wasn't based on something as flimsy and fleeting as a feeling? What if love wasn't defined by desperation or even passion but rather by giving and choosing?

What if I were to tell you that youds could have a real love that isn't just based on chance, fate, feelings, fantasies, or luck? What if I told you that you could have a love that is unconditional, deeper than feelings or attraction? A love that doesn't depend on a flower petal hanging on for dear life. A love that never fails. That's the love everybody wants—and it is achievable.

Many of us have lost sight of what real love is. We have believed the lies of the media and accepted the tainted picture that Hollywood paints. If we base our definition of love on an ever-changing culture, we're going to stay confused. If we use our own emotions as a standard for love, they will continue to fail us. We will never feel the security we crave if we try to build it on the quicksand of today's version of love. But what about a love that is never changing, never failing, and never leaving? Isn't that what we all want?

Before we can truly recognize this real love, sometimes it helps to view the wrong love.

> We will never feel the security we crave if we try to build it on the quicksand of today's version of love.

## WRONG LOVE

When I was in high school, I was in a relationship with a guy that I was over the moon about. He was a few years older than me, and I thought he was *the* guy. You know the kind: The guy the other girls wanted. The guy with relationship experience. The guy the other guys were jealous of.

I was just happy to be his girlfriend. But something about our relationship didn't sit right with my mom. She prayed daily about it.

One night she came into my room after I had fallen asleep and happened to see my phone on my bed. When she picked it up, it was unlocked, and a message popped up from my boyfriend. She clicked on it and read, "I can't wait for you to start driving. Now we can be together all the time and have more privacy." When she read that message, she felt alarmed. She knew this relationship needed to end . . . and soon. But he and I spent every waking second talking, either in person or on the phone. So, her prayers picked up tenfold. She prayed one specific prayer over and over, knowing it would take a miracle for the relationship to end: "Lord, remove all desire for him from her heart. I pray she would become disgusted by the sight of him!"

Bold, huh? Yeah, that was my mom's actual prayer.

One day not long after, I came home from school sick. Have you ever had your throat swell up so much that you can't swallow? That's how this started, and it was horrible. I couldn't eat, and I was in so much pain. I was tired and weak all over and had no energy to talk to or see anyone. My doctor diagnosed me with mono. I stayed in my room and slept. A week later, my boyfriend came over to bring me a smoothie. I don't know what happened—and I wish I could describe to you exactly what I felt in that moment—but all I can explain is that every bit of attraction to and desire for him had vanished.

Feeling nothing but repulsion, I broke up with him as soon as I got better. When I got home from school after my first day back, my mom asked about him. I just said, "Ew. We broke up. I couldn't do it anymore." I think it's safe to say it was all due to the prayers of Mama Prew. My mom and I joke about it now, but that day I learned the power of prayer! Prayer changes things.

Although my mom's prayer helped end that particular relationship, I was still obsessed with boys. I realize now that this obsession started when I was a little girl. I wanted love so badly. I watched *Cinderella* and dreamed of my prince. I listened to Britney Spears and longed for a man I could sing about. I lay in bed at night and practiced my reactions when I would get my first kiss.

It goes without saying: For most of my life, I've had to fight the temptation to put my worth and value in having a boyfriend. I believe I did this because it was a tangible hope—one I could see. But even when I did get the guy, it still left me empty and unsatisfied.

*The love you hope for and long for won't require you to settle for a person or rush a season.*

I now know the love you hope for and long for won't require you to settle for a person or rush a season.

I now know I was looking for the right kind of love in the wrong places, which made it the wrong kind of love. Because . . .

The right kind of love with the wrong person = the wrong love.
The right kind of love at the wrong time = the wrong love.

## FAKE LOVE

I've always been one of those people who actually *listens* to the lyrics of the music they're playing. Back in my high school days, I'd blare the artist Drake in my car. Even though I don't do this now or agree with everything Drake has ever said in his songs (even the clean versions), he seems to understand what it's like to experience fake love:

> I've been down so long it look like up to me. . . .
> I got fake people showin' fake love to me
> Straight up to my face[2]

It's crazy to think that we sometimes intentionally seek out fake. I shopped for my first knockoff purse in Chinatown in NYC. I remember so many details: the smell of the streets, the crowded sidewalks I clumsily navigated, and me rocking some blue eye shadow and thinking I was the star of my own movie. Being fifteen without a job, I knew there was no way I would be able to convince my dad to buy me a two-thousand-dollar bag, but I had a good chance of convincing him to buy me a knockoff one for forty-five dollars! Playing the daddy's-girl role perfectly, I charmed my way into a "Yes, you can buy the bag."

One shady exchange with a stranger in the back of a bodega later, I got the bag. I felt so cool! I took pictures with it. I started taking it to school every day. I felt like *the* hot stuff. Until one day when I was walking with a bunch of my friends in the hallway and the handle broke in half. They all started laughing and I was so embarrassed. When I got home and told my sisters, they replied, "What did you expect? It was fake. Fake doesn't last long!"

Looking back, I wish I'd spent more time considering the implications of their words. If I'd saved up for a real designer bag, I would have had to save for years. *Why wait for the real thing when I can settle for a fake one that looks similar?* This is also how many of our minds work when it comes to love and relationships, even unknowingly. Why do we so often settle for a knockoff version of real love? Is it because it's easier? Because it doesn't cost as much? Because we can obtain it faster? We settle for a less-than version of what we could have because maybe we are tired of being alone, we are tired of waiting, or we fear we might not find anything better. But you don't need more of what you've been settling for; you need something that will last.

Sometimes it's hard to discern between what's real and what's not. Social media makes it easy to fake: Fake your looks, fake your mood, and fake your relationships. I know people who will post photos of themselves smiling with their boyfriends—making it seem like a perfect relationship—who at the same time are crying themselves to sleep at night because things really aren't going as they seem. And then they break up a month later.

I've seen countless influencers, bloggers, and celebrities post photoshopped pictures of themselves with heavy filters, creating a beauty and lifestyle standard that is impossible to achieve in real life, even for them. With the help of technology and heavy makeup, we can make anything look real, even if it isn't. I know, because I used to do it too—all of it. Photoshop, filters, planned photo ops. I'm not proud of it, but I, too, have joined in the fake social media ploys.

Take, for example, when I was filming a reality TV show and had a massive pimple pop up on my face—one I couldn't hide. No, it was there to make its presence known. Well, once the show finished filming and it began to air, there was this photo of me with that massive pimple on my face. I loved the photo minus the pimple, so I thought, *Well, I can easily take care of that—Photoshop!* I went in, erased that pimple off my face like it had never been there, and posted the photo on my social media.

Only to discover that, an hour later, the TV show posted the same photo *without* erasing the pimple. I started getting countless DMs and tweets calling me out for photoshopping my pimple. So genuine and real of me. Safe to say, I learned my lesson. It's better to be pimple-faced and real than to showcase fake perfect skin.

Many times over the years, I talked about how fake social media can be . . . but then the same day proceeded to post filtered photos. Maybe this doesn't seem like a big deal, but it bothers me when everyone wants to talk about a problem yet no one wants to be the one to do anything about it. In this case, everyone likes to talk about the false reality social media paints and the negative effects it has on consumers, but then everyone continues participating in the very thing they condemn. That hypocrisy left me feeling convicted, so I texted my friends and committed to posting only non-filtered photos from that day forward.

Social media isn't the only way we can become disillusioned. Through music, movies, and shows, we've become de-sensitized to what's real. The lyrics of songs and the scenes on TV are just as capable of convincing us that lies are truth. I'm not here to scare you or to tell you to get rid of technology—I use it too—but I am here to bring truth and hopefully aware-ness. It's through ignorance that we fall for and settle for fake love. And honestly, a lot of people will be fooled. But they will continue to see that fake love won't last.

So, what are we to do? How do we avoid fake love? I think we should start by acknowledging the phoniness. When we feel ourselves longing for something we've seen or heard, we're capable of saying, "That isn't real life," and coaching our minds and hearts with the truth. For me, truth is God's words and standards.

It's time for us to be the exception, to stop complaining and start changing. Maybe you need a break from social media. Maybe you need a no-filter commitment. Maybe you need to change the type of music you're listening to or what you're watching—even if it's just for a period of time. If you don't like what you've been getting, do something about it. If others are okay with settling for a knockoff version of love, let them! It doesn't mean you have to. As for you and me, we are destined for God's best.

One of my favorite books about love, *Love Changes Every-thing*, says,

Falling in love with fake will always leave you frustrated, especially when it comes to fake love. There are numer-ous kinds of fake love that will catch your eye and that you can pursue. But there is only one love that can radically and unapologetically tear down the filters of your heart and carry you until your last breath. There is only one love that can take away the urge to settle for anything less than all that you are called to be. There is only one love that can step into the darkest of nights and light up your whole life. There is only one love that violently repels fake. This love—real love—changes everything.[3]

*We weren't made to settle for fake. We were made for real love, a lasting love.*

## REAL LOVE

My mom used to write notes to put in my lunch box—even through high school. She didn't want me to forget her love for me, even for a second. Every day, there would be some form of encouragement ending with "P.S. I LOVE YOU—Mom." The notes meant the most to me when I didn't deserve them or expect them—times when I was maybe rude to her or didn't show her much affection or appreciation, yet she still went out of her way to let me know that she loved me. It made me wonder, *What have I done to deserve love like this?*

Receiving her unconditional love brought me to a place of overwhelming gratitude. My mom was always there for me and always believed in me, even when I couldn't see anything in myself. She would tell me she loved me and why she loved me, and she would remind me of who I am and what I am called to do. She showed me what real love is: A love that never withholds. A love not based on my response or performance. A love not based on feelings.

I remember the first time a guy ever told me, "I love you." It scared me and I ran away. Granted, I was only five, but that didn't change even when I was nineteen. But when I finally found the right love, I didn't run. I didn't hide. I accepted it and welcomed it. I remember when my now-husband, Grant, told me he loved me for the first time. We had been dating for only a couple of weeks. He was driving me home from a rehearsal dinner, and he pulled over on the side of the road. After he parked the car, he sat there staring straight ahead for a few minutes. Then finally he turned to me and said, "I can't take it anymore, Madi. I know it feels soon, but I can't hide it. . . . *I love you.*" With any other guy, this was when I would look off in the distance and then pat him on the shoulder and say, "Thank you!" But this felt different. This felt *real*. This felt *forever*. With a racing heart and sweaty palms, I grabbed his arm, looked him in the eye, and shared, "I love you too." It was the first time I had ever said it back in the moment.

Our relationship is far from perfect. We have ups and downs. Good days and bad days. Moments of questioning the other person. We had our moments of praying, "God, is this your will?" and following up with "Are you sure?" But amid the hard moments and changing seasons, one thing we can say with confidence is this: "God brought it, God was in it, and God was for it." It isn't easy, but it is real. It isn't perfect, but it is real. It isn't a Hollywood movie, but it is real. It is real love.

The kind of love you may have heard about before. The kind of love that makes me want to be more like Jesus. The kind of love that pushes me closer to who I want to be. The kind of love that empowers me to make a difference in the lives of others. The kind of love described in 1 Corinthians 13:4–8:

> Love is patient, love is kind. It does not envy, it does not boast, it is not proud. It does not dishonor others, it is not self-seeking, it is not easily angered, it keeps no record of wrongs. Love does not delight in evil but rejoices with the truth. It always protects, always trusts, always hopes, always perseveres.
>
> Love never fails.

Love is patient and kind? Love is selfless and others focused? Love isn't reactive or resentful? Love trusts, protects, and hopes? That kind of love is bigger than you and me! And that kind of love is greater than what we can give on our own. That's why real love doesn't come from another imperfect human. The love you've been looking for doesn't come from a compliment, a like, a follow, a boyfriend. Real love is found only in relationship with God. He is the love you want.

I know what you're thinking: *Madi, you just finished telling us how Grant's love is real love . . . and now you're telling us that only God can offer us real love?* Okay, so you're right. Sort of. The love between Grant and me is so powerful and fulfill-

> The love you've been looking for doesn't come from a compliment, a like, a follow, a boyfriend. Real love is found only in relationship with God.

ing and real *because* Christ is at its center. He's the foundation we've built our entire relationship on. I know that sounds kind of ambiguous—and *very* churchy. Let me try to explain it with another metaphor.

If you've ever been under the authority of a coach or director, you know how important it is that the person in charge knows what they're doing. You rely on them to help you—to teach you. They're your leader. I had a softball coach once who was about to retire. To say she was checked out of the experience would be putting it mildly. She never had our lineup ready, and half the time, she called us by the wrong names. Even the officials calling the game would sometimes look at her in bewilderment, like, *What are you even doing?* Although we were a talented team, we had a losing season.

To try to make a relationship work without God as its leader is like playing for a bad coach. You have no direction other than your fallible, culturally influenced human minds. And even though we are well intentioned, we don't know how to love each other well. We don't know how to love like 1 Corinthians 13 tells us to love. We need a leader—a coach. We need someone to look to in times of doubt, times of conflict, and times of temptation to make us better than we would be on our own.

That's why figuring out where you stand with God matters so much when it comes to loving others. Cultivating a connection with him is what sets you up to be successful in healthy relationships. Getting to know his character by reading his words and spending time with people who know him well helps you become more Christlike and, as a result, more loving.

Let me reiterate—what Grant and I have isn't perfect. But the leader of our relationship *is*. When we do get selfish or impatient or angry, we have a standard of love to look to that helps us make better choices in how we speak to and treat each other. This is true in dating *and* in friendships.

One of the wonderful ironies of learning to give and receive love in a relationship with God is that once you've established a firm foundation of who you are in God's esteem, finding a romantic relationship doesn't feel quite as pressing. You aren't as needy or desperate, because you've been completed by the realest love of all—the love of the One who created you.

Do you want to experience that love? It's the greatest decision I've ever made, and it's based on what Jesus did for you and me on the cross. If you haven't ever made that decision, take a moment, put this book down, and talk to him. Tell him your disappointments, your pain, even your anger toward who you think he is. He's not scared of your doubts or questions. I want you to experience the same love that I do with God, because only in that relationship will you find all the answers you've been looking for and fulfill all the longings you've been living with.

He wants to have a relationship with you. Yes, *you*. Maybe the reason you picked up this book is that he's calling out to you to stop striving and to surrender to his love. With him, you don't have to ask, "Does he love

> I want you to experience the same love that I do with God, because only in that relationship will you find all the answers you've been looking for and fulfill all the longings you've been living with.

me? Even after all I've done?" The answer will always be "He loves you. He loves you always."

> We know and rely on the love God has for us.
> God is love. Whoever lives in love lives in God, and God in them.
>
> —1 John 4:16

## BONUS CONTENT

Using your smartphone,
scan the code for bonus content.

waterbrookmultnomah.com/the-love
-everybody-wants-chapter-2-bonus-content

# 3

## PICK ME

### Know Your Worth

> *What do they have that I don't?*
> *Will I ever get picked?*
> *What do I have to do to be chosen?*

Sororities are a big deal in Alabama, where I went to college. There's a week before school starts called rush, when sororities are introduced to students. Over the course of the week, sororities decide which girls they want to join them, and students decide which sorority they want to join.

I had all my outfits ready for rush. I wasn't worried—I was confident in my accomplishments. I had worked hard throughout high school, graduated with honors, and performed more than seventy-two hours of community service. I was also proud of my achievements in sports: four-time state champion in basketball, two-time MVP, and Player of the Year nominee.

There were two sororities at the forefront of my mind. My

friends and I had discussed it beforehand, and those were the ones we had decided on so we could be together. I thought, *They have to pick me!*

The week was long and tiring, as I had the same conversations over and over again, but I was excited and hopeful. The day finally arrived when I would get the card back from the Panhellenic rush committee. This card would list the five sororities that wanted me. From there, I would write out the top three sororities I wanted, in order of preference. But when I received my card, I thought there must have been a glitch in the system.

Neither of the sororities I had planned to be in with my friends was listed. *Ouch.*

I replayed the week in my mind. I thought everything had gone great. I was shocked and hurt. I texted my friends, "Did you get the two sororities we talked about?"

"Yes!" they replied. "Did you?"

I felt a deep pit in my stomach. *They got picked and I didn't.*

Bid day came (the day you find out what sorority you're in), and I was in an arena full of girls screaming with joy as they found out which sorority they got. As I stood, staring at my envelope, I couldn't help but still feel rejected. All the other girls began to sprint toward their sorority home, and I was left standing there confused and embarrassed.

The thing is, I loved the sorority that chose me. I adored the girls. Under any other circumstances, I would have been one of the girls jumping up and down and running. My disappointment had everything to do with not being picked by the same sororities that chose my friends. What did the girls who got picked have that I didn't? Why had they succeeded where I failed? Why did it feel like I was never the one getting chosen?

My mom texted to ask how I was feeling. She was on her way to meet me at my new sorority home. The truth was that I was beginning to believe the lie that because I'd been rejected and my friends had been accepted, I was somehow less valuable and had less to offer. While everyone else was out celebrating, I was crying in my mom's lap.

"Madi," she said, brushing the hair off my snot-smeared face, "I know you know this, but it might help if I remind you. Everything happens for a reason. God has a plan for you."

I nodded. "Mm-hmm."

"And you *did* get chosen," she said.

As usual, my mom was right. I nodded.

As the months passed, I grew to love the girls in my sorority and began to develop a heart for them and a close bond with them. Throughout that year there were many opportunities for me to encourage and love the girls around me, which opened my eyes to ministry. I started serving at my church, which ultimately led to my decision to join their Bible college. As I look back now, it's obvious that what felt like a deep rejection in the moment was really a blessing—one that played a major role in leading me to my purpose.

Through not getting picked by the group I thought I wanted, I was led to put my confidence and hope in God, not in a sorority or in the opinions of other people. But that realization didn't come overnight. It didn't even come over weeks. It would take years for me to understand just how valuable *not* being picked would turn out to be. At the time, it felt like another one of the many rejections I'd experienced.

Have you ever had a moment like this when you felt like you weren't picked? What my mom reminded me is true for you, too, right now, whatever you're going through. You are picked. Because the God who created the heavens and the earth and everything in it has chosen you by name and has made you in his image. And only by knowing and believing that truth can we begin to understand our worth in him.

## THE PICK-ME CYCLE

I wish I could tell you that I no longer struggle with wanting to be picked or wanting to be the first choice, but I would be lying to you. I still sometimes feel like I'm drowning in a never-ending sea of unworthiness, desperate for a breath of air, and to be honest, I don't always turn to the right things for that breath.

This cycle has played a role in just about every area of my life: my relationships, my job, my friendships, and more. In the pages ahead, I will tell you about how I continue to wrestle with this—but more importantly, I will tell you how God continues to rescue me from my insecurities.

## DON'T BE A PICK-ME GIRL!

Maybe you've seen a girl trying to gain attention on social media, and someone will comment, "Stop being a pick-me girl!" Or maybe you've seen it in real life. Maybe a friend has totally changed her look, her likes and dislikes, and even how she talks and acts to get attention or affirmation. Maybe, like me, you've been a pick-me girl yourself.

When I hear the phrase "pick me," I don't immediately think about social media and people suggesting that a girl is just thirsty for attention. Honestly, I think about middle school PE class. You know the moment I'm talking about—when the PE teacher picks two team captains, and the rest of the students must sit there, waiting and hoping to be picked. The captains alternately call out names of the people they want on their teams . . . and there you sit, thinking, *Ooookay. Is anybody ever going to pick me? There are only ten of us left. What if I'm chosen last? What if no one wants me? Oh no. Now four people left. Oh gosh. Please, somebody, choose me!*

Tell me I'm not the only one to have gone through this.

Have you found yourself in a place where you so desperately wanted that guy to notice you? You did everything you thought you needed to do to get his attention. You wore tighter clothes, you posted the hot pics, you even physically gave yourself to him . . . but he still didn't choose you.

Or maybe you haven't ever felt like you're enough in your family's eyes, so you did everything to get that "Way to go" or "I'm proud of you" or "I love you." Maybe you've just never felt good enough at anything, so you keep performing and striving for that acceptance and belonging.

I'm pretty sure none of us want to be a pick-me girl. But how often are we waiting for someone to choose us and affirm us? Maybe you're waiting for that job you always wanted to land in your lap. Maybe you're waiting for an invitation to a party or for someone to swipe on your profile or for your crush to finally notice you.

I get it. I've always had to wrestle with this. *Will I make the team? Will he choose me? Will I get hired? Will they include me in their hangouts?* Being a pick-me girl is exhausting. And it robs us of so much. It robs us of peace. It robs us of contentment. But it also robs us of *time*—our most precious commodity. If you're always standing around, waiting to be picked, you may miss out on the meaningfulness of life or even the purpose you've already been chosen for.

Sometimes when people attempt to break free from the pick-me cycle, they go to the opposite extreme and think, *I don't need anybody. I will never give my heart away, because no one deserves it. I am all I need.* I want to be clear: That is not the message I believe, live out, or am here to encourage you with. That mindset will only leave you alone yet still feeling the same emptiness as before. You may think having those walls up keeps out all the bad, but it also keeps out all the good. It will cause you to miss out on the abundant life God has for you.

When we long for superficial acceptance, we're leaving our fate, happiness, and security in the hands of other people. We're allowing those who don't even know who they are to define who we are. Sometimes we will even shift who we are and what we're about for people whose lives we wouldn't necessarily model our own after. We don't always do this consciously either. We'll see someone else get attention for something—how they dress or what they spend their money on—so we'll do the same things, even if that's not really us. And we do this because we aren't confident in our own identity. Some of us have no idea who we really are, because we've been so busy being what we think will get us the most affirmation and attention. In other words, we've lost our sense of self.

Do you value yourself? Or do you only hope others will? Why should someone else give you what you don't even give yourself? The more you value something, the higher your expectations are of how it's to be treated. It's time to start placing a high value on ourselves. Not desperate, but confident. Not striving, but secure. And don't worry—we're going to be talking a lot more about this as we go on!

But here's where it starts: It's time to discover how valuable we truly are, because only then can we walk in the fullness of all God has to offer and who he has called us to be! We must learn to love ourselves so we can truly love the one life we have to live on earth and so we can give love to the world around us.

## GET YOUR OWN JACKET!

Have you ever gone shopping with a mission? By that I mean, you head to the mall with an hour to shop and a picture on your phone of *the* item you're looking for. Yet as you shop around, you find everything except the one thing you need. Why does it feel like this happens to me all the time?

You may remember this story from my last book. I went shopping at Forever 21, where I was looking for this specific jacket that I really wanted.[1] After looking around for a long time, I couldn't find it, but I did find a bunch of sweaters and sweatshirts I liked. When I walked into the dressing room to try them on, hanging on the hook inside was the coolest jacket I had ever seen. *Destiny. It was meant for me.*

I could have picked any dressing room, but I had chosen this one. And the jacket I wanted was right there waiting. Now all I needed to do was make sure it fit. I tried it on. It fit like a glove. *Could this be more perfect?* I forgot all about the other clothes and decided I would make only one purchase that day. I chose to keep the jacket on to show it off. When I walked out of the dressing room, I noticed a girl staring at me strangely. At first, I thought, *Oh, she's jealous of my jacket—I would be too!* But she kept looking, so I became a little nervous. I asked her if everything was okay, and she said, "Well, you walked into my dressing room, and now you're wearing my jacket."

I don't think I spoke for a solid three minutes. I felt so awkward. I took off the jacket and slowly handed it to her. We ended up laughing and joking about the situation, and I eventually found a similar one.

I tell this story a lot when I speak, because it's the perfect picture for a common human tendency: *How often do we try on other people's lives because they look better than our own?* We like what they have—the Insta-worthy house, the cool job, the Prince Charming, the big following, the perfect family. We want those things for ourselves, and we think, *Her life is so much better than mine, so I'll just try to be her.* Maybe we feel the pressure from society to compromise who we are, and we think that if we wear *her* "jacket," we will finally be accepted or feel like we're enough.

Or maybe it's a situation where we aren't trying to wear other people's jackets but people keep placing jackets on us. And these jackets look like other people's labels and expectations. At this point, we look in the mirror and we don't even recognize ourselves. We don't even know who we are anymore.

When I came off reality TV, I felt intense pressure. I was bombarded by so many opinions and judgments. Words were thrown at me that I wouldn't dare repeat—some of the meanest things you've ever heard. It would have been easy for me to succumb to those words or feel the pressure to change myself and my convictions to be more accepted or liked. It would have been easy for me to fall back into that moment of young Madi in the bathroom stall. But during it all, I had people around me who reminded me of who I was and encouraged me in my purpose. It wasn't always easy, but I chose to walk confidently in that, even with opposition around me.

This pressure to conform, to compromise, to compete and compare threatens who we are at our very core, and if we aren't quick to catch ourselves, we can easily be shaped into people we didn't plan on becoming. I don't want to see a generation of girls and young women who have been pressured to perform or prove their worth, who are living unaware, just following the next trend, and who don't even have their own voice anymore.

What about you? Do you feel it too? Have you ever been overwhelmed with the pressure to be someone else? So much so that you've lost your sense of identity? Maybe you feel you've lost the special thing that makes you *you*, or you feel you're the same as the next girl?

In the same way my mom and my friends have my back when I feel under attack, I want to encourage you to keep on being you. I want to remind you how special and unique *you* are.

You see, there will be a lot of obstacles to overcome as we learn to fight for our identity and love ourselves. Pressures, questions of purpose, and misplaced sources of identity can get in our way. Just as I stumbled into someone else's dressing room, we can get stuck staring in the mirror, wearing clothes and lives that don't belong to us. But it's time to see the beauty within ourselves. It's time to "wear our own jacket" proudly! It's time to know who we are and what we have to offer.

Until we learn to love who we are, we won't be able to experience true contentment, freedom, and confidence. We won't be able to receive other people's love to the degree we were designed to. We won't be able to love other people to the degree we desire to. Until we love ourselves well, we can't expect to be loved or to love others well. The only way to be truly confident and secure the way you crave is to realize who you belong to. In knowing who you belong to, you realize who you are. In realizing who you are, you know you have nothing to prove, so you don't need the validation or acceptance of other people, because you already belong.

> Until we love ourselves well, we can't expect to be loved or to love others well.

Do you know who you belong to?

I can't separate my confidence and security from knowing who I belong to—and that's God. The more I grow in my relationship with him, the more confident and secure I become. As I study the Bible, listen to his people, and spend time talking to him, my thought processes become healthier, my heart becomes less dependent on external affirmation, and I feel more at ease with who I am.

Look, I don't know where you stand on the topic of God, but for me, belonging begins and ends with him. I believe I am created by God on purpose *for* a purpose. I believe that about you too. Maybe you're not there yet—maybe you aren't sure about the whole God thing. If that's you, I'm glad you're here. There's a ton in this book that applies to you the same as it would apply to anyone else. But if you aren't sure who you belong to or why you're here, that's where you need to start.

## THE LOADED QUESTIONS

When we struggle with our sense of belonging and identity, we may torture ourselves with some loaded questions. See if any of these feel familiar.

### 1. Am I Hard to Love?

I can't tell you how many times throughout my life I've asked myself if I'm hard to love. In other words, *Is there something wrong with me?* It seemed like everyone around me paired off with long-term boyfriends so easily. Then, in my early twenties, all my friends started getting engaged. Weddings and baby showers followed, and I felt like there was a secret to finding love that was eluding me. Because I felt different from those around me, I immediately began to doubt what was inside me. I thought, *Maybe they have something I don't.*

I thought maybe there was some reason everyone else was getting picked to become girlfriends, fiancées, and wives. Maybe there was something undesirable about me. Something that screamed "Don't pick her!" or a label across my forehead that told everyone to keep looking. I carried this perspective for a long time, questioning my own worth because other people didn't seem to be able to see it. I based my value on other people's acceptance of me. If I had to guess, you've done that, too, at some point in your life. Maybe you're even doing it right now.

Instead of asking, *Am I hard to love?* we should ask, *Do I have a hard time loving myself?* For so many of us, the rejection we've experienced feeds the lie that we are no longer worthy of love from others. But what's really happening is that somewhere along the way we've stopped loving ourselves and started believing we are unworthy. I've learned over the years that the questions *Am I hard to love?* and *What's wrong with me?* have less to do with how others view and accept me and more to do with how I view and accept myself.

Learning to love yourself means that you don't change yourself to be like someone else. You don't compromise your values, convictions, standards, and likings to make someone else feel comfortable or to fit in with those around you. You don't cave to other people's expectations of you.

Loving yourself isn't born from fear and people-pleasing, nor is it born from pride and self-centeredness. It's born from a place of belonging, assurance, rest, and contentment. And if we learn to view ourselves the way that God views us, we don't long for acceptance and belonging; we love from acceptance and belonging. Read that again. We are not longing for belonging; we are loving from belonging. Loving yourself well means being confident no matter the circumstances, giving yourself grace when you mess up, cheering on others when they succeed, speaking words of life over yourself even when you don't feel it, and loving those around you.

In working through this and learning to love myself, even with my unique quirks and talents, failures and weaknesses, and loud and strong personality, *I've learned how to be confident in who I am by being comfortable with who I am not.* We must learn to accept that even

> *If we learn to view ourselves the way that God views us, we don't long for acceptance and belonging; we love from acceptance and belonging.*

though we may look different, think differently, and dress differently from those around us, being different isn't a bad thing. Being different is what sets you apart and makes you special. Who wants to be normal? Normal is too common and too easy.

## 2. Am I Enough?

I've come to discover that in striving to be who we *think* we want to be, we lose the power we could have in embracing who we already are. When we bend ourselves to fit into someone else's mold, we become ineffective. Another truth is that we aren't ever going to feel like we're enough based on external standards. If we try to be, we will constantly be living off the highs and lows of other people's acceptance or our own performance, predicating our worth and value on external, uncontrollable, inconsistent factors.

I longed for something steadier, more constant. I longed for my confidence and view of myself to be unwavering, no matter what was going on around me. After I got my heart shattered in high school, I knew I had to do something different. I knew I couldn't escape hurt forever—that would be an unrealistic goal. But I also knew I had to change the way I perceived myself—Madi. Madi at face value. Madi with no makeup, no awards, and no boyfriend. *That* Madi needed a new measuring stick, because the one I had been using left me feeling worthless and unlovable.

One new habit I started was to pay attention to my thoughts about myself. Anytime I began thinking negatively about who I was or telling myself how dumb I had acted, I stopped those thoughts before they could take root in my mind and heart. I began to reject the constant condescension I treated myself with. After all, I would never talk to another person the way I was talking to myself, so it had to stop.

Instead, I started reminding myself of what I was good at. (Be forewarned if you try this practice, because it can feel a little uncomfortable at first.)

*Madi, you are a good friend. Madi, you are loyal. Madi, you make your family proud.*

But more important than what *I* thought about myself was what God thinks about me, so I also began reminding myself of what God says about Madi.

*God says I am loved (Romans 8:38–39). God says I am wonderfully made (Psalm 139:14). God says I am worthy (Luke 12:6–7). God says I am chosen (John 15:16). God says I am enough (Ephesians 2:8–10).*

It may not come naturally at first—it takes practice. But

replacing lies with truth over time rebuilds our brains and re-wires our hearts to not rely on the world (or on guys) to find the love everybody wants. Because we already have that within ourselves—if we're willing to do the work to build those relationships within.

Left to my own thinking and my own will, I am not enough. But God within me is. He is more than enough. This means those mistakes you've made, the things that have happened to you, the experiences of being rejected, the times someone walked out on you, the moments of watching everyone else be happy, and the seasons of heartbreak that left you questioning "Am I enough?" don't define you and can't hold you back from who you're becoming and where you're going. With God, we are loved, chosen, and full of purpose. And we can say with confidence, "Because of God, I am enough."

### 3. Will I Ever Be Picked?

Before I started college, I thought it would be a good idea to compete in a pageant. I'm not exactly sure why. I guess it was another pick-me moment where I wanted to excel and be affirmed. Looking back, I can say pageants are not my thing, but hey, at least I tried!

I got all my dresses and necessities for the pageant. I worked with a pageant coach to learn everything I didn't know—which was *a lot*. Quite frankly, I had no idea what I was doing. I was going in hopeful but ignorant. A lot of girls dressed to the nines, hoping their beauty and status would win them the title. I found a girl who seemed to also be confused about everything going on, and I walked up to her, grabbed her hand,

and said, "We're going to be friends." Thankfully, we got paired up to room together!

The next few days were nothing short of uncomfortable, but I stayed confident and hopeful. Competition day arrived, and my friends and family all came out to support me. The part I was the most nervous about was walking in heels. I was a basketball player. I didn't wear heels. Yet I mustered up the courage, did the initial walk on the runway in front of the judges and crowd, and thought, *Wow, that wasn't too bad.*

After my walk, I made my way downstairs to the dressing room to change into my evening gown. I looked at myself in the mirror and hyped myself up. I said a few prayers. I rehearsed the walk, making sure I wouldn't get my heels caught in my dress. Next thing I knew, my one pageant friend came down yelling, "Madi! Where have you been? You just missed your swimsuit walk!" *Well, great. There goes my chance at placing.* I knew my mom and dad were thinking, *Where is she? We spent a small fortune on a swimsuit just for her to miss her walk?* I'm sure the judges were confused when they called my name and no one walked out.

I laughed and said, "Well, I guess I still gotta finish this thing." So, I went out in my evening gown when it was time and just had fun with it. But still, I couldn't get over the fact that my friends and family came to this pageant to watch me, and my parents spent all this money on me, only for me to miss my swimsuit walk because I was in the dressing room hyping myself up. Iconic.

I wonder how many times I've done that—how many times

I've been so focused on the act of performing that I've missed out on moments of experience. How often have I been so preoccupied by the wrong things that I've been distracted from my goals and purpose? We live in a world that gives us ample opportunity to look any direction besides straight ahead. But that's where our focus is the most helpful—the most needed. Being present in the *right now* of our lives is critical to experiencing life fully.

My friend and I stood beside each other when they began calling out the girls who placed. I wasn't surprised I wasn't called. When the pageant ended, my friend and I hugged each other and laughed. I said, "I don't think pageants are our thing." She nodded in agreement.

I looked at my parents and said, "Can we please go eat some doughnuts?" I was so happy it was over and I could finally eat whatever I wanted again!

It's safe to say I understood why I wasn't picked, and even though it was still a little embarrassing, I realized the role I played in it. I have several friends who are in the pageant circuit, and they are incredible at it. It wasn't the pageant; it wasn't the judges—it was me! Sometimes we are quick to blame other people for our insecurities or feelings of unworthiness when we should look at ourselves a little more closely and pay attention to the role we might have played.

Thankfully, though, God isn't sitting up on a chair made of clouds, looking down, watching our every move, and picking us based on our performance. He doesn't pick us based on our looks or efforts. So many of us are striving and straining, just hoping and praying someone will acknowledge and affirm us, when, in reality, we have already been picked. We were already chosen when we were created and placed on this earth.

Again, I don't know where you stand on the topic of God and if you believe you are his unique creation, but I would encourage you to take those doubts or curiosities to the Bible—or to a believer you know and trust who can answer your questions or point you in the right direction.

Yes, you were chosen. You were chosen before you were even created (Jeremiah 1:5). And, yes, you were made for love—the love of the One who created you.

> Because true belonging only happens when we
> present our authentic, imperfect selves to the world,
> our sense of belonging can never be greater than our
> level of self-acceptance.
> —Brené Brown, *The Gifts of Imperfection*

## BONUS CONTENT

Using your smartphone,
scan the code for bonus content.

waterbrookmultnomah.com/the-love
-everybody-wants-chapter-3-bonus-content

# 4

# IF HE WANTED TO, HE WOULD

## Know What You Deserve

> *Why do guys treat me this way?*
> *Is it really settling if he loves me?*
> *After all I've done wrong, do I still deserve to be loved?*

We all have unspoken expectations for what dating should be or for what a guy should do in a relationship. But so often, those expectations aren't met, and we are left disappointed. Maybe you've heard, "If he wanted to, he would!" meaning that if a guy *wanted* to demonstrate his love for you, he would do it. So by default, if those expectations aren't being met—if he isn't showing his love for you—maybe he doesn't love you.

But we need to reexamine our logic. A better way of thinking is this: If he values you, he will. In other words, if a guy isn't showing his love for you, maybe he doesn't value you! You carry something incredibly valuable and worth protecting: your heart. And if a man values your heart, he will demonstrate that appropriately. *Want,* in this case, communicates convenience and is about self. *Value* communicates service and is about the other person. You see, we are created for so much but often settle for little! We have to know what we are worth so we don't settle for less than the best version of our lives.

Over the last few years, there's been a lot of talk about knowing our worth. For example, I just did a hashtag search on Instagram, and there are more than 4.2 *million* #KnowYourWorth posts. As I scrolled through them, I wasn't surprised to find that most of the messages pointed to the idea that worth comes from within ourselves. Meaning, because we demand to be treated as worthy, we are worthy. And men are to show us our worth by buying us nice things and treating us like goddesses.

Listen, I love gifts. Who doesn't? And I love how Grant treats me like I'm the only woman in every room. But relationships—healthy ones—are built on an equal partnership. This doesn't mean one person gives 100 percent and the other gives nothing. It doesn't even mean both give 50 percent. No, both need to give a full 100 percent. There is mutual value and respect. And our true worth—our value—comes not from ourselves or even from someone else but from a God who loves us relentlessly and pursued us to the cross and beyond to trade his Son's life for ours.

If you're not familiar with the story of Jesus's death and resurrection, do a quick search for John 3:16–18. (I especially like The Message translation.)

See, our worth isn't found on an Instagram page, in a job, or in how we make a guy treat us. Our worth comes from the cross, where Jesus traded his perfection for our flaws. We are worthy because we are *his*.

Knowing our worth comes back to having a whole relationship with God. Because on our own, outside the love and grace of God, humans are pretty messed up. We do some awful things to one another. I know I'm not naturally forgiving, gracious, or generous with praise. By nature, I want Madi to feel good 100 percent of the time! It's only through knowing that my value isn't earned or lost on my own merit that I understand that being worthy has nothing to do with anything Madi has done. It has everything to do with who Madi is at her core—a child of God.

If my identity is found anywhere else, I'm likely to base my worth on how other people—especially men—treat me. I'll think that if a guy is treating me well, I'm worthy and valuable. If a guy is treating me like crap, I'm not worthy nor am I valuable. Even if I post a photo of myself and tag it #KnowYourWorth after dumping someone who did me dirty, that doesn't mean I understand my own value. Knowing your value, believing your value, and living as if you are valuable comes from using God's standards for what a healthy, loving relationship looks like. Because I know who I truly am and where I stand with God, it feels unnatural for me to be treated poorly by a guy or a friend. And it feels unnatural for me to treat

> Knowing your value, believing your value, and living as if you are valuable comes from using God's standards for what a healthy, loving relationship looks like.

others poorly too. I won't stand for either. *That's* the freedom and power of knowing where our worth comes from.

So, if you want to know who someone really is, look at what they value. I've been in relationships where I didn't feel valued and I felt like I had to beg for the bare minimum—bare minimum respect, attention, and expressions of love. And let me just set the record straight: We should never have to beg for scraps of love. I've learned over the years that you don't have to negotiate your way into a heart that values you. I refuse to make someone a priority in my life who doesn't make me a priority in his and treats me only as an option. In other words, I refuse to be with someone who doesn't value me. Love and respect are not wants, which are based on feelings. Feelings come and go. So, if he is led by his wants, one day he could be filling your room with roses and candles and another day he could be cheating on you. Feelings can't be the foundation of a relationship, partly because they can't always be trusted. Values are secure and stable. Values like honesty, integrity, a good work ethic, empathy, wisdom, and generosity. If someone embodies these traits in their everyday life, they'll be reflected in how they treat you—in how they love and respect you. Find someone who values action over intention.

## TO BE VALUED, KNOW YOUR VALUE

When you don't know the value of something, you don't tend to guard it to the extent that you should. And when we don't know our personal value, many of us give away our hearts like we're a Black Friday 60-percent-off sale and then wonder why we aren't treated like we're Gucci. Listen to me: When you know your value and what you're worth, you don't offer it for free or at a discount. *When you know your worth in Christ, you don't have to play hard to get; you just are hard to get.*

As women, our goal shouldn't be to turn heads but rather to gain respect. It shouldn't be our figures and looks that attract male attention but rather our hearts and minds. Because if your body is what gets them, it's your body that must keep them. That's exhausting. And what happens when a better body comes along or they settle for a fantasy on their computer screen? I think you know the answer.

Girls who are unsure of their value so often feel the need to change who they are and what they need for a guy to like them. But truthfully, it's possible for a guy to know every square inch of your body but not know *you* at all. Does he know what makes your heart cry? What makes your heart leap? What your greatest dreams and desires are? What makes you feel most loved and seen? When we don't understand our value, we will convince ourselves of almost anything. "He probably fell asleep." "Maybe that *was* his cousin texting him." "He loves me deep down—he just doesn't know how to show it."

No. If he did, he would.

## GREAT EXPECTATIONS

One of the biggest things I've learned is this: Unrealistic expectations break hearts. Healthy expectations uphold standards. There is a big difference between unrealistic expectations and high standards. One is based on fairy tales and culture's skewed picture of love, and the other is based on desiring a love that will last. (And let me just say, all expectations are unrealistic if they aren't communicated.)

*Unrealistic expectations break hearts. Healthy expectations uphold standards.*

I was in a relationship once where I had a full-on meltdown because my car door wasn't opened for me. I slung harsh comments like, "My dad always opens my mom's door! I guess he loves her more than you love me. I guess he's more of a man!" I continued on and on, trying to get a rise out of him. I don't know why I felt so hurt by such a small inaction, but I made sure to let him know how it made me feel.

One day he turned to me and said, "Madi, you're always looking at what you're not getting, but do you ever look at what you're giving? You expect so much but give so little!" *Ouch.* That was a wake-up call for me. *What do I do with that? Is he right?* If I'm being honest, he was. I always expected the other person to do everything for me, to go above and beyond, while I stayed at arm's length. Sounds unfair, huh? It was. But it was easier to be loved than to give my love and possibly get rejected. I didn't know how to let anyone in, because what would happen if I gave my heart to them and they didn't choose me? I had no understanding of my worth—my value.

My friend Tara dated this guy who lived three hours away from her. He'd *never* make the drive to see her. He'd expect her to come to meet him, then let her drive home at all hours of the night without ever checking that she made it home okay.

My friend Danae had a boyfriend who would openly mock her any time they were in a crowd. Later, he'd be sweet and lovey-dovey behind closed doors, but in public, he was no more than a bully. I have another friend who dated a guy for *two years*, and he refused to post photos of them together. He'd post about his dog, his boat, and his truck, but he wouldn't recognize her as his girlfriend on social media.

Other friends have put up with even worse scenarios. I've witnessed my friends getting body-shamed, cheated on, and emotionally abused. I've watched time and time again as women excuse their boyfriends' unacceptable behavior by saying, "All men are this way" or "This is just how it is." Everything inside me wants to shake them and scream, "No! That's not how it should be. That's not real love. There is so much more!"

Listen, you don't have to be a princess or a pushover. Define your deal breakers and hold steady. Don't let anyone make you feel crazy for vocalizing and upholding high standards. But at the same time, check yourself. Are you giving as much as you're taking? Are you treating the guys you're dating like *they're* children of God?

## SETTLING FOR LESS

If you've read my first book, you may remember this story— the story of the sparkly pink bike.[1] I'm retelling it here because it's a core memory for me and I can't *not* discuss it when I'm talking about value and worth.

Do you remember your first bike? I remember mine like I got it yesterday: hot pink with sparkles, a white cushioned seat, a cute white bell, and tassels. It came with a matching sparkly pink helmet. I waited patiently for this bike. Every time we passed by it in Walmart, I would turn to my mom or dad and point with excitement: "This one! This is the one I want!" Weeks went by, and I didn't get my pink bike, but I kept holding on to hope! Christmas rolled around, and I bet you can guess what was sitting under the tree on Christmas morning. That's right—my pink bike!

I didn't even look at the rest of the gifts under the tree. This was the one thing I'd asked for and desperately had to have. Of course, it still had the training wheels on it. My friends would come over every day and bring their bikes. We would often vote on who had the best bike—mine would always win. I was so proud of it and loved to show it off. It was the best gift I'd ever received. Months and months passed by, and I still got home after school and ran to hop straight on that bike.

One day my dad came home from work and asked if I would give my bike to my younger sister Mallory for her birthday. I was taken aback that he would make such a request. This was the best gift he'd ever given me! But I couldn't say no to my dad. I looked up at him and said, "Daddy, anything but my bike. She can have my new American Girl doll or my new toys for the dollhouse." But he insisted that she needed the bike. At first, I walked away upset and frustrated. How could my dad ask me to give up something so precious to me? After taking the night to think about it, I woke up the next day and called my dad into my room. When he came in, I handed him my pink helmet, and with tears in my eyes, I said, "She needs it more than me, so she can have it, Daddy."

My dad smiled big and told me to follow him. When I followed him out of my room, he led me outside to the most beautiful bike I'd ever seen. It was bigger and shinier, and it had no training wheels!

I rushed up to my dad and hugged him tightly. "What did I do to deserve this?" I asked. I'll never forget his response. He told me, "You gave up good for best."

Even though I didn't understand why my dad, who loves me so much, would ask me to give up something I loved, I trusted him. I trusted that my dad knew more about what I needed than I did. So many times I haven't given God the same level of trust and submission! And how much more does God in heaven know about what is best for me? Instead, there have been times that I've held on to what I thought was valuable when God was trying to offer me something better. I've settled for less.

Valuable things are worth waiting for. They really are. So often we take good enough in place of best because we are shortsighted, impatient, or lacking in self-awareness. There have been many moments when I wanted to cling to what I had, even when I knew it wasn't God's best for me. There have been many moments when settling or compromising seemed easy or comfortable. How about you? Are you holding on so tightly to harmful or unnecessary relationships, habits, or activities that it seems impossible to let go? Are you settling for good enough when you could have God's best?

Maybe you've settled in life. In your job. In your family. Or in your relationships. But I am here to encourage you: Okay is not who you were created to be. Good enough is not good enough when God's best is available to you. Getting by is not where you belong. A life of more is your destiny.

Many of us keep trying to make it work. We think, *Oh, it's not a big deal to have to settle in some areas. Everyone does. I can make it work.* But let me tell you, you can't get your abundantly more by settling for less. And in the same way, you can't get God's peace and promise if you're holding on to the problem. You can't dance with confusion and expect clarity. Many of us never get the abundantly more God has for us, because we aren't willing to go through what it takes to get there.

*You can't dance with confusion and expect clarity.*

Here are four of the most common reasons we settle.

## 1. We Settle Because We're Tired of Waiting

We get impatient when something takes longer than expected or is more difficult than we thought it was going to be.

You've undoubtedly heard, "Patience is a virtue." But sadly, that's not one of my innate personal virtues, because *I hate waiting*. I hate waiting for the light to turn green. I can't stand waiting in long lines for coffee. I get impatient waiting on the confused person in front of me to figure out what they want to order. I want to *go now*. I want to *act now*. Maybe you find yourself here. Maybe not literally in one of those superficial scenarios, but maybe you are waiting for a promotion, for God to reveal your next step, or for that guy to finally ask you out. Waiting can be hard and lonely. It can feel like a wasted season. And for some of us, we get so tired of the wait that instead of remaining steadfast in valuing ourselves and turning down good for best, we settle out of impatience. Or we become fixated on the things we want to change about our lives and take our eyes off our relationship with God and ourselves. We complain, become bitter, and have a hopeless perspective and attitude.

## 2. We Settle Because We Don't Believe We Deserve Better

So many people believe they are unworthy of the best. *Everyone else is smarter than me, skinnier than me, prettier than me. No wonder they got the job, husband, platform, opportunity. They are just better than me; they deserve it.* Why do we do this? Sometimes it's because of our own insecurities, which are rooted in a lack of understanding our own worth and value. Sometimes it's because we carry shame from past mistakes and trauma. We think, *No one would ever choose me. Look at what I've done, and look at where I come from.* So, we settle for whoever will give us time or attention, even if their love isn't the love we truly deserve or desire. Yet we convince ourselves that it'll have to do, because we don't want to risk being alone.

## 3. We Settle Because We Feel Pressure

When I graduated college, so many of my friends were getting married and I was newly single. I tried not to compare my season with theirs, but it was hard when I felt so much pressure. Everywhere I went, I would get asked, "Any new contenders?" or "Got a new boo?" or "Did you find a date for the wedding?" It made me feel like, as a single, I wasn't enough. It made me feel like there was something wrong with me since I hadn't found my person yet. Even though I was only twenty-two at the time, it made me feel like I had to find someone, even if I had to settle. And then maybe, just maybe, I would stop getting asked all the annoying questions about my love life and I would finally have a date to the hundred weddings I was in. I hadn't even hit my mid-twenties, but it felt like the clock was ticking. My singleness was like a weight on my shoulders. At times, it was heavy enough to make me want to settle.

When our circumstances don't match our hopes, desires, or God's promises, we feel the pressure to give up, give in, and settle. Especially when we feel like we are running out of time or others are getting ahead of us. In dating, marriage, jobs, or having kids, we can feel pressure from our family, society, school, or spouse, or even from ourselves, to have it all figured out and to be on some timetable. When things don't happen when we think they should, we end up settling because we think it's better to have something than nothing.

## 4. We Settle for What's Safe

We often settle for what's comfortable, easy, and convenient, because of fear—fear of the unknown, failure, or rejection. We take the easy and safe route because then maybe we're less likely to get hurt or to fail. Whether we lack discipline, perseverance, or courage, many of us settle for what's comfortable. I've had moments of ignoring my intuition or red flags because I was afraid of how uncomfortable and unfamiliar it would be if I paid attention to them. I feared what other people would say. I feared getting rejected. We often settle for what's safe, even when we know it's not God's best.

And the lie many of us continue to believe? *This is just what it is. And this is how it will always be.* But I have good news for you: There is hope. We can believe a different narrative. We can choose to live out the life God has for us.

Ephesians 3:20 talks about God being "able to do immeasurably more than all we ask or imagine, according to his power that is at work within us." The part of that scripture that stands out to me is "according to his power." That should bring us such relief. *We* don't have to do anything but have faith, because it's on God to deliver. But if we settle—if we don't wait on God's best—we're exchanging what he can do with his infinite power for what we can drum up with our limited human power.

> There is hope. We can believe a different narrative. We can choose to live out the life God has for us.

If it were up to many of us, yes, settling would be our destiny. But don't reduce God's promises to what makes sense to you. Don't let what you don't have talk you out of what could be yours with patience and trust. There will be many opportunities and temptations to settle for good enough. Your thoughts will tell you all the reasons it's not going to happen for you. *I'm too old. I'm too young. I'm too broken. My past is too messy. I don't have the talent or resources.*

You have to be intentional and say, "I got hurt, but I am not going to drown in self-pity." "I've been wounded, but I am not going to be bound by bitterness." "I've experienced loss, but I refuse to sink into despair." You have to keep running, persevering through the painful and lonely nights and the waiting seasons. The *best* awaits you if you just don't settle.

> *The best awaits you if you just don't settle.*

We started out talking about the idea that *if a guy values you, he will.* He will love you appropriately. And that's true. That's important. You shouldn't settle for anything less than that. But I want to finish this chapter by reminding you of something even more important: *Because God values you, he will.* He will always be there. He will always love you. He will always forgive you. He will always choose you. He will always pull through. You will always be worth pursuing and protecting. So, it's time for you to believe it.

Now, what about you? If God chooses to love you, do you also choose to love yourself? To value yourself? *If you value yourself, you will.* You will believe you are worthy of love. You will believe you deserve abundantly more. You will see yourself the way that God sees you. You will treat yourself with honor, respect, and love.

> Live from the abundant place that you are loved, and you won't find yourself begging others for scraps of love.
>
> —LYSA TERKEURST, *Uninvited*

## BONUS CONTENT

Using your smartphone,
scan the code for bonus content.

waterbrookmultnomah.com/the-love
-everybody-wants-chapter-4-bonus-content

# 5

## HE COMPLETES ME

Only Jesus Can Complete You

> *Who am I without a boyfriend?*
>
> *When will someone come along to fill this emptiness in my heart?*
>
> *Am I more than my relationship status?*

When I hear someone say, "He completes me!" a red flag pops up in my mind. To me, this implies that we think having a significant other makes us more of a whole person than we otherwise would be. Listen, I've been there. I've felt "less than" because I didn't have my person yet. But this is problematic for a lot of reasons. If we are always operating from a place of lack, we are going to grasp at everything we can, trying to hold on to stability, security, and feeling valuable. And that often means we find our identity in our relationship with another person. So, what happens when that person fails you or lets you down?

We weren't meant to enter a relationship as half a person.

No relationship will be strong or healthy unless both people are whole. The healthiest and strongest relationships are strong before they ever even begin. Let me say it another way: *A partner in life is meant to complement you,* not *complete you.* Before you can be ready for another person, you have to be made whole all on your own—through your relationship with God and your relationship with yourself.

Let me tell you about the time I was a bit obsessed with this boy in high school. I had a crush on him for a while, and he wasn't making a move. So, I started feel-

> The healthiest and strongest relationships are strong before they ever even begin.

ing insecure. *Does he like someone else? Am I not enough?* I tried all the things. I got my friends to talk me up when I wasn't around. I got my guy friends to ask him in the locker room what he thought about me. I wore my cutest clothes. I played hard to get but still a little flirty. No matter what I did, I couldn't get a read on this guy! Oh, and I should clarify: This isn't how I encourage you to find out if a guy likes you, but this was the way my fifteen-year-old mind worked.

One day my friend and I decided to take a ride around the neighborhood in my hot pink golf cart. (I was too young for a car, and everyone in my neighborhood drove golf carts . . . and mine happened to be my favorite color at the time.) My crush lived in our neighborhood, so we thought maybe we could just innocently drive by. We continued doing this every day after school. Stalkerish? For sure, but we didn't care.

On one of those afternoons, I'd had all I could take, and I told my friend to drive this time. I sat in the passenger seat, cranked up the radio, and belted out the words to Taylor Swift's "You Belong with Me" with the confidence of someone *much more* musically inclined than I am.

Truthfully, I don't know what exactly I was hoping to accomplish, because I knew if he saw me, I would be so embarrassed. But there was this little part of me that hoped he would. As we drove by one last time (the third time that day), I was belting my heart out . . . and the back door opened. He walked out and made eye contact with us. My friend got so nervous that she drove straight into their mailbox.

He rushed over to check on us and ask what happened. We tried to explain without sounding crazy, but there wasn't much of a way around that. We just were crazy. I'm pretty sure that the whole time we were talking to him, my face was bright red. We apologized for the damage and inconvenience, and he assured us it was okay and not a big deal. I couldn't believe it. We drove off and started dying laughing. I said, "I guess I deserved that!" Talk about embarrassing. That was one of those moments that I wanted to rewind and redo.

It was like God's way of telling me to stop being boy crazy. But I didn't listen. Months later, I was in English class and my teacher pulled me aside and told me, "Madison, you are a good writer, but you could be a great writer if you weren't so boy crazy." Was my distraction *that* obvious? Apparently. His words stung, but he wasn't wrong.

Unfortunately, it still took time for me to realize how much my obsession with love and relationships and attention from guys was affecting my life. I had centered everything on men and what they thought about me. *What does a man want? What will make a man fall in love with me? What can I do to get that man's attention? When will I meet my husband? How much more fulfilled, content, and whole my life would be if I met my Prince Charming!* I dreamed of a guy who would sweep me off my feet and make me feel loved. I dreamed of a happily ever after.

I wish I could just blame rom-coms and Taylor Swift, but the truth is, *I* fueled my obsession just as much as anyone or anything else did. My mindset was skewed. I was looking for a man to complete me.

## COMPLEMENT, NOT COMPLETE

When it comes to relationships, we live in a world that constantly tells us we need to find our partner to be truly happy. I mean, how many movies do you watch where there's a strong, independent single woman who, at the end of the movie, is still unattached? The message is clear: A happy ending is a romantic relationship with a partner. I don't know about you, but I don't want *just* a happy ending. I want to find contentment and meaning through all seasons and stages of my life. I want that for you too.

Yes, we were made for love. But for far too long we've defined that love as the love of a man. Yes, finding the right person does add so much goodness to your life—I'm not going to pretend that it doesn't. Grant has added so much laughter, joy, and fulfillment to my life in ways I hadn't thought possible. But that's the point: He's *added.* He hasn't *completed.*

Here's a healthier ideal: complementing. A complement is

an independent but appreciated addition. It says, "I don't need you in order to be whole, but I want you because you add value to my life." *Completing speaks to lack, but complementing speaks to addition.*

With a healthy perspective and with the right attitude, we can view a relationship as something life-giving and good that we desire. But we also understand that no person is going to be able to make our hearts feel healed, whole, or complete. We see that relationships are made up of two imperfect people, so there will be hurt, misunderstanding, risk, and possibly even loss. Relationships are the most beautiful things that we have on earth. So, they are worth fighting for. When we are healthy, we know who we are, why we were created, and the value we have to offer. We are not desperate and dependent on someone else to prove our value to us.

If you depend on someone else to complete you, how can you ever be fully you? I've seen so many of my friends change for another person's acceptance and love. I've watched as they transform themselves completely in a relationship, centering their identity and purpose on the relationship itself. This change resulted not from their own convictions or desires but rather from someone else's preferences or pressure. Granted, as women, we crave security and we want to be desired and loved. That in itself isn't the problem— after all, God created us that way purposefully. But God's intention was never for a boyfriend or even a husband to fill that void. Only someone much bigger can do that: God himself.

> *If you depend on someone else to complete you, how can you ever be fully you?*

I have an order of importance for my relationships. First is my relationship with God. For me, my identity, purpose, contentment, and joy are all rooted in my faith. With or without a romantic relationship, I'm confident in who I am and what I'm called to do, and I'm content in where I'm going and who I'm becoming along the way. Security isn't found in a spouse. Security is found in a Savior.

Second is my relationship with myself. I've learned that if I'm not at peace with Madi, I will always be searching, striving, and straining. I've learned how to invest in myself well and how to live from a place of abundance, not lack.

Third is my relationship with others. Finding community—people that I can laugh with, grow with, and suffer with. People that will cheer me on, fight for me, encourage me, make me better, and hurt with me when I'm hurting. Romantic relationships fall into that third category. My relationship with God comes first. Then the relationship I have with myself. Then I'm able to love my significant other from a healthy, abundant place.

Why? Because I'm already complete. I'm whole. I'm happy. Things aren't perfect—I still have hard times and challenging days. But overall, things are steady. I don't have to be a chameleon, changing myself based on what I think someone else wants. I have the freedom to just be me—Madi. Madi, who is loved by God, accepted by God, and valued by God. Madi, who not only loves herself but also likes herself. Madi, who has value and standards.

When you build on a foundation *that* strong, there's nothing about you that needs completing.

## "YOU'RE MY EVERYTHING"

In the past, I dated this guy who had a lot of charm, style, and status. He had the coolest outfits and was well liked by everyone, especially women. Girls would flood his DMs and throw themselves on him. Even though he wanted me, I still constantly felt pressure to fit this mold of what I thought he would want. I felt pressure to dress a certain way so he would call me beautiful or to make sure that I kept his attention on me and not any other girls.

My mom finally called me out on it. She told me she noticed that I was acting and dressing differently. At first, I was defensive. "No, I'm not. What are you talking about?"

But even as I denied it, I felt the hot flames of shame creeping up my spine. Slowly but surely, I was becoming less like myself and more like who I thought I needed to be to keep his attention. In fact, when I looked back on my dating history—which had actually been maybe three serious relationships—I saw a pattern of me becoming more like the guys that I was with, for better or for worse.

I'm sure at some point in your life you've felt this tension too. You so desperately wanted a guy's attention that you changed yourself to be more like what you thought he would want, even if it cost you something you deeply cared about. Some of my friends who always valued purity have ended up giving themselves physically to a guy because they thought that would keep him around and maybe then they would feel chosen and seen by him. Then when the guy walked out or cheated, it made them question what they did wrong and why they weren't enough.

If that's your story, I'm so sorry. I hurt with you and grieve with you. But I also want you to know that you can do something different. You can draw a line at this point in your life, step across it, and start over with a renewed mindset. No, you can't go back. But moving forward down a new and healthier path can start *right now*.

How have we gotten to the point where, as women, we let men change us, then leave us and break us? I'll tell you how. *We have a poor view of self and an idolized view of romantic relationships.*

Let me say it like this: Your purpose is not a person. Your identity is not a relationship. When we make someone our everything, we lose everything else. We continue looking for divinity in humanity. Doing so leaves us with insecurity and anxiety because humanity is broken, unable to meet our deepest needs. When we put our everything into something that is fallible, it's going to let us down. Instead of making someone your everything, make them important, but don't lose yourself in the process.

> When we make someone our everything, we lose everything else.

So, how do we do that?

## 1. Keep Your Routines and Habits

I've spent a lot of time thinking intentionally about what's important to me. I value my quiet time with God in the morning. I value working out and eating healthy. I value spending time with people who make me better and call me higher. I value keeping a clean space around me. And I value learning and reading.

What about you? I challenge you to make a list of things *you* value and want to commit to. Write out those routines and habits that are important to you. Decide how you want to invest in your body, soul, and spirit. Note how each thing on your list can make you spiritually, physically, mentally, emotionally, and relationally healthy. So, next time that guy calls you and wants to hang out, don't compromise, settle, or blow off the things you value. Don't change them just because they don't fit the routine or likings of that guy you're interested in. And if you're currently in a relationship or hope to be one day, have this list nearby so you can check it constantly, making sure that you aren't compromising in the areas of your life that fill you up, make you happy, and set you up as a powerful individual.

## 2. Keep Your Passions and Purpose

What are you passionate about, and what are you good at? Usually, those things combined equal *purpose*. The things I'm passionate about are communicating (both writing and speaking), loving those who feel unlovable, and challenging people to be the best they can be and helping them get there. These natural inclinations combined with the affirmation of others in the same areas makes me confident in my purpose!

Now, what about you? What gets you up in the morning and makes you feel alive? What is something you've done that others have affirmed? Combine those, and that's your purpose! For those of you who still aren't completely sure, that's okay. But you should at least have an idea of what you enjoy and what comes naturally to you. If not, now is the time to explore that. Ask your friends and family. Do some introspective journaling. Try new things. Your purpose can be accomplished only by *you*. So, it's important to grow in awareness.

Your purpose is your baseline for decision-making and direction. Your purpose is the guardrail on your road through life, keeping you on the right track and away from the dangerous shoulders of aimlessness and misdirection.

The people in our lives either add to our purpose or subtract from it. They either encourage us in our calling or pull us away from it. That goes for friendships and romantic relationships alike. If you want to be a motivated and ambitious person, find motivated and ambitious people to spend time with. If you want to chase after your purpose with all your energy, find someone who is doing that in their own life.

If you find that all your energy, plans, and good feelings rise and fall on what makes someone else happy, you've made a person your purpose. If that's true for you, the best-case scenario is that you will delay your true purpose, waste your time, and end up with regret. Why? Because you will never be satisfied to sit on the sidelines, forfeiting or neglecting the very reason you were created by God. The right person should propel you even further into your God-given purpose, not make you question or neglect it.

> The right person should propel you even further into your God-given purpose, not make you question or neglect it.

## WANTS AND NEEDS

I'm probably not the first person to tell you there is a big difference between *wants* and *needs*. Wanting to be in a romantic relationship isn't a bad thing and can even be healthy. I did and I do. I wanted a boyfriend. I wanted someone I could confide in and partner with. I want my husband.

But thinking you need a boyfriend/partner/husband isn't the same thing. I cringe at the number of times I've watched a rom-com and heard the words "I need you!" I've also sat across the table from many women as they've expressed that they need a man. I always try my best to be careful how I respond, because I never want to crush their hopeful spirit. But truthfully, when we think we need someone else, we are relying on them to complete us. When we feel joyful, peaceful, secure, and loved only when another person meets our needs, we are in trouble. Desperation and neediness aren't signs of a healthy relationship. (And aren't especially attractive either.)

As we've discussed, many women feel that if they're not in a relationship, if they haven't yet found their husband, or if they haven't been asked out on a date in a long time, they're "less than." They believe there must be something wrong with them. Deep down they believe the lie that they need a man to feel complete and whole. Whether that message is coming from society, family, or even church, it often convinces us that if we don't find a man by a certain age, there is something wrong with us and we have less to offer the world.

So often, while men grew up playing with dinosaurs and fire trucks, watching movies of cars blowing up and such, women grew up playing house and watching *Cinderella*, which teaches that only if her prince finds her glass slipper can she escape her life of bondage and step into her destiny. Or *Sleeping Beauty*, which teaches that only if she gets a kiss from her prince will she live. Historically, women have been trained to believe we *need* a man. But no human being will ever be able to meet the needs of your heart.

After we got engaged, a friend asked Grant, "How did you know Madi was the one for you?" Of course, he took the opportunity to flatter and affirm me in many ways, but what really stood out to me was him saying, "She didn't need me. She just wanted me." He went on to explain that in dating me, he saw a woman who found her full confidence, security, and satisfaction in Jesus, not in him. It gave him the freedom to be the man God had called him to be, not the man I *needed* him to be. As you know by now, this wasn't always my story. And it might not be yours right now. But I pray that it will be. I pray that you won't put all your hope in finding a husband and all your prayer into getting a partner. And that if you do meet your special someone one day, your heart and eyes will be set on Jesus as the only one you need.

I believe that a heart can be made whole and complete only by the One who created it. Anything else—a hookup, a relationship, money, followers—will satisfy for a moment. But when those fail you—and they will—they leave you more empty and broken than before. My heart has been made whole because I've found the only One who can satisfy and complete it. Thankfully, I'm no longer driving by guys' houses singing Taylor Swift songs, desperate for love and attention, needing someone else to complete me. I now have healthy relationships, and I'm no longer looking to others to fill in the blanks of my life.

My purpose isn't a person. It's so much bigger than that. It's bigger than me. It's my God-given assignment that only I can fulfill. And you know what? You have a God-given assignment too. Your life is no accident. Your life was designed with intention. It's only in living out our purpose in Jesus that we are ever satisfied. It's only through knowing *his* love that we are complete.

> The LORD is my shepherd, I lack nothing.
> —Psalm 23:1

BONUS CONTENT

Using your smartphone,
scan the code for bonus content.

waterbrookmultnomah.com/the-love
-everybody-wants-chapter-5-bonus-content

# 6

## LOVE IS BLIND
### Red Flag Alert

> *It'll get better once we get married.*
> *He'll change. I see potential!*
> *My expectations are just too high.*

I almost ran over my neighbor's cat.

I was driving after a long day of work and didn't have my glasses on. I was pulling into my neighborhood, and a big rock appeared to be in the middle of the road. I didn't think much of it until I saw this "rock" moving. I slammed on the brakes and, thankfully, barely missed Mr. Whiskers.

When I told this story to a friend, she mentioned I should look into LASIK eye surgery. LASIK is a procedure where a laser is used to change the shape of your eyes to improve your vision. At first, I didn't feel like my vision was *that* bad. Maybe things were a bit blurry and I couldn't read faraway signs, but was it that big of a deal?

But after doing some research, I realized I was a good candidate for the procedure. I didn't know just how bad my vision was until after I had the surgery. Let's say I was blown away by the results. I was *amazed* at the clarity. I wasn't squinting anymore, and I could even see the individual leaves of trees, when before they'd just been big green blurs! My vision was finally as it should be.

When it comes to relationships, we tend to have selective vision. We see what we want to see. Seeing things that might contradict who we want a person to be? Nah. We'd rather those things just stay blurry. You may have heard the saying "Love is blind," insinuating that we are blind to the other person's negative tendencies. We focus on their potential instead of looking at patterns displayed in their everyday life.

Why do you think we make these excuses for the people we're with? I think it often comes down to fear. We're afraid of the cold, hard truth. We're afraid of what is on the other side of accepting that truth. We're afraid to be alone or rejected. I know I've feared the unknown. Even though it's scary, it might be time to ask the difficult questions of your relationship and speak the truth in love—even if that truth leads you somewhere you don't want to be.

## BLIND TO WHO THEY ARE

You've heard the term *red flag* before. A red flag is a negative behavior or mindset that likely indicates a larger problem.

The red flags you tolerate or ignore at the beginning lay the groundwork for the kind of relationship you build. If he never leaves his phone unattended and hides the screen from you when he's texting, it's not a guarantee that he's shady, but it is a red flag indicating that he might be. Some red flags are obvious—they're more like flags that are on fire. And some red flags are subtle—they take time to emerge. Both can be equally harmful to the future health of a relationship.

Let's look at seven common red flags that I've seen either in my own relationships or in the relationships of others. While you read, ask yourself if you've seen

> The red flags you tolerate or ignore at the beginning lay the groundwork for the kind of relationship you build.

any of these red flags in your own relationships. (By the way, the red flags discussed below aren't to be used only to evaluate another person; they are also for you to evaluate yourself.)

## Red Flag 1: He Isn't Healed from His Past

If a guy isn't healed from past relationships, hurts, or addictions, it will create obstacles in your relationship and likely have a negative effect on you. If he isn't fully healed from his last relationship, he's just looking for a Band-Aid—for a fill-in. He is choosing not to deal with the pain he really feels and is just trying to escape it with another relationship (you!).

If the relationship starts off heavy with a lot of baggage, it will just continue to get heavier because baggage doesn't disappear. Usually, more collects and keeps piling up. You want to have a relationship with someone who makes you better but also makes your life lighter. Besides, you deserve way more than being someone's rebound.

One indicator that a guy isn't healed from his past is continued communication with his ex. I've seen this dynamic in my friends' relationships before. They'll excuse it by saying, "Oh, they're still friends. He's a really nice guy." Let me just say that there are very few *good* reasons for your guy to have any ties to his ex. In fact, outside of having a child together, I really can't think of any. If he's calling up his ex or tracking her location or bringing her up constantly—in a negative *or* positive way—it's very unlikely that he has healed from that relationship. And if he grows defensive, secretive, or deceptive when you ask a question about his past, he's got baggage that you don't want or need to take on.

## Red Flag 2: Your Values and Beliefs Don't Align

You and the guy you're dating should both be pursuing a relationship with God independent of each other. A guy believing in God isn't enough to make a relationship work. Owning a Bible doesn't equate to a growing relationship with Jesus. Just because he wears a cross necklace doesn't mean he is living for God. You want a man whose faith runs deep, from the inside out. Not the other way around.

So many of us have a desire to rescue, fix, and change someone. It's like we want our own hero love story. We romanticize the idea of being the one they changed for. But I firmly regard this as true: If they don't change for God or themselves, they won't change for you. You need to be partnered with someone who believes what you believe and who has a life mission aligned with yours.

You can't build a secure home on two different foundations. You can't build half your house on sand and the other half on concrete and expect your house to withstand the storms that life will bring. So, if you're trying to build a life with someone whose foundation isn't the same as yours, it won't withstand the pressure of time. If you and your spouse have the same theology, attend the same church, and practice your faith at home, statistics indicate your chance of divorce is dramatically reduced.[1]

> *You can't build a secure home on two different foundations.*

## Red Flag 3: You Are Dating for Who He *Could* Be and Not Who He Is Now

Don't date someone's potential. Don't date someone that you hope will change. If he isn't doing it now, what makes you think he will do it later?

The ability to see who someone might be in the future is a gift. But it becomes dangerous when it's your heart and destiny on the line. Is he changing for you? If so, it's likely going to stop as his security in your relationship grows.

> *If he isn't doing it now, what makes you think he will do it later?*

If he is trying to become better for you, he might become bitter because of you. Over time, resentment can take root, and he'll see you as a taskmaster and a nag.

If a man is making changes in his life because he wants something better for himself or, better yet, for God, it's beautiful and it will last. So ask yourself, *Does he do these things only because I tell him to? What is his motivation? Does he have a genuine desire to be better for the right reasons?*

> *Relationships don't change people; they reveal people.*

Relationships don't change people; they reveal people. Pay attention to what's being revealed.

### Red Flag 4: There Isn't Respect, Peace, or Trust

If you don't have peace about the relationship and you find yourself constantly defending or making excuses for your partner, let me just tell you bluntly: It's not God's best for you.

Ladies, if you don't respect him enough to follow his decisions and convictions or if you don't trust his relationship with God enough to be led by him, he's not the one for you.

If he is playing games with your heart and toying with your emotions, you deserve better! The constant swing between emotional highs and lows isn't healthy. And having a healthy relationship isn't boring. People confuse toxic with fun and passion. There is nothing fun about a lifetime of instability and a lack of trust and peace. It will end up sucking all the energy and life out of you.

> *There is nothing fun about a lifetime of instability and a lack of trust and peace.*

If you are constantly wanting to check his messages and social media notifications and wondering if he is talking to other girls or cheating on you, consider ending that relationship right now. Either he isn't the man for you, or you aren't ready for a relationship. Trust and respect are foundational in relationships. That isn't something that you "figure out later."

## Red Flag 5: Everyone Around You Disagrees with the Relationship

If you have healthy friends and family, a faith community, and good accountability around you, listen to them. They will tell you the truth, even if you don't want to hear it. Pay attention to their comments, *especially* if you don't like what they're saying.

If everyone who cares about you questions or disapproves, lean into that. Don't be quick to get defensive or angry. Ask questions. If they really care about you, they're saying those things not to hurt you but to help you. Remember, sometimes the people around us can see things we can't see.

Both of you in the relationship should have mentors, accountability, and a church community in order for the relationship to be as strong and healthy as it should be. If you lack those types of relationships, that should be your next step. Find people who are maybe one or two seasons ahead of you, who have stable, healthy lives you admire, and ask them to be part of your circle. I've had to move outside my comfort zone to pursue some of my most life-giving relationships with mentors and leaders. But I'd never be the person I am now without them and their advice and wisdom.

## Red Flag 6: His Behaviors Don't Align with His Beliefs

I don't know who first said this, but it's the absolute truth: Sometimes their behavior is the only answer you need. This red flag should be *huge*!

*Sometimes their behavior is the only answer you need.*

A person's behavior will follow their beliefs. If they truly believe God should be the priority in life, their routine and decisions will follow that belief. If they truly value you and purity, their behavior and boundaries will reflect that belief.

I'm a big believer in action over intention. Anyone can have good intentions, but if those intentions aren't followed with good actions, they're meaningless. Just because someone can "talk the talk" doesn't mean they're a quality person. And just because they mean well doesn't mean they're right for you.

Everything a person does should be led by their beliefs: how they talk, how they dress, how they make decisions, how they spend their time and money, who they surround themselves with, etc. One of the best aspects of Grant's character is that he doesn't even have to tell me his values and priorities, because they're evident in his everyday life. Someone led by a strong belief system and strong convictions is someone worth following. Otherwise, don't trust them, and definitely don't follow them.

## Red Flag 7: If He Isn't Teachable and Willing to Grow

Nothing turns me off more than a complacent or apathetic spirit. Someone who doesn't want to grow and get better. Someone who is content with mediocrity. Or someone who is too prideful to admit they have areas where they need to grow. *Yuck*. I was raised in a house with a teacher and basketball coach, so there was no room for complacency, and we strove for excellence. My dad would always say my sisters and I had to give 110 percent in everything because 100 percent wasn't enough.

When someone isn't willing to work hard for something, in my opinion they don't deserve it. If they aren't willing to work for the relationship, they don't deserve the relationship. If they aren't willing to work for you, they don't deserve you.

So, remember, when someone shows you who they are, *believe them*. Don't ignore the red flags. Lean into them. Listen to them. Trust your gut.

*If they aren't willing to work for you, they don't deserve you.*

Love doesn't have to be blind. You can have the kind of love you really want, with eyes open. The kind of love that can't be lost. The kind of love that always wins. That's the love you and I were made for.

> When people show you who they are, believe them
> the first time.
>
> —MAYA ANGELOU

**BONUS CONTENT**

Using your smartphone,
scan the code for bonus content.

waterbrookmultnomah.com/the-love
-everybody-wants-chapter-6-bonus-content

# 7

## IN MY FEELINGS

### Emotions Make Bad Leaders

> The heart wants what the heart wants, right?
> If it feels right, doesn't that make it right?
> If I can't trust my heart, what can I trust?

There was this one time I told my dentist he was hot.

Let me explain. I had just gotten my wisdom teeth removed, and I was a bit out of it. At school, people were talking about this really cute dentist, and he was the one doing the extraction. He was young with dark, curly hair and perfect teeth (of course!). I made sure to look good the day of my procedure because I knew Dr. Cutie would be there.

My mom drove me to my appointment and warned me that they would give me laughing gas and that it might make me feel a little loopy. I didn't think much about that part, but when I started to breathe in that laughing gas, secrets started flying out! I'm *pretty* sure I made some comment about his looks to him before I dozed off. As soon as the surgery ended and my mom came to get me, I began saying out loud to her, with the dentist right next to me, "Mom, did you see my dentist? He's hot!"

My mom laughed and encouraged me to save all my comments for the car ride. I proceeded to yell out my number and told the dentist to give me a call if he wanted to. My mom was laughing and blushing, embarrassed but amused by my carefree spirit. I had no problem with sharing my feelings and thoughts while on that laughing gas. I spoke about what I saw. I shared what I felt!

When I got in the car, I started sharing a bunch of secrets with her and confessed that I had sneaked out of the house a few times without her or my dad knowing. She couldn't believe all that she was learning! A few hours later, when the sedation effects wore off, I was reminded of all the comments and secrets I had shared, and I was ashamed that I could be so careless with my words and actions. How could I be so out of control and led by whatever I felt without even pausing to wonder, *Should I say this?* or *Is this appropriate?*

I look back on that time and laugh now, because not only did I tell my dentist—who happened to be married with kids—that he was hot but I also shared so many personal things with my mom and was so impulsive. I joke that my payback came the day after the surgery, when I had a bad reaction and my face got so swollen that I had to wrap a bandana full of ice cubes around it to reduce the swelling.

Even though it's a funny story and every now and then I will look back at those pictures when I need a good laugh, it reminds me of how often I can be so impulsive and reactionary. Maybe not in a literal sense, where I'm blurting thoughts out uncontrollably, but I can often lack deliberation in how I live—by choosing my words, responses, and actions all based on how I feel in the moment. I've learned how dangerous this can be, because I later find myself down a road of shame, regret, and resentment, wondering, *Why did I do that?* or *Why would I say that?* or *How did I get here?*

Are you ever driving and you zone out for so long that when you arrive at your destination, you wonder, *Wait—how did I get here?* That happens to me all the time—not just literally in the car, but also in life. How about you? Do you ever look at your life and have no idea where you are or how you got here? You've just been "driving along" and now here you are.

Maybe you aren't proud of the decisions you've made, and you feel so much shame. It torments you, but you keep it inside because you don't want others to know the amount of guilt and embarrassment you're carrying. But you keep asking yourself the same question over and over: *How did I get here?*

The truth is, we don't just wake up one day far from our identity and purpose, saying, "I think I'm going to waste my life by chasing meaningless things!" It's a slow process, and little by little, we let our lives be directed by emotions instead of values and priorities, leading to a dangerous destination.

Have you ever said, "I'm going to start waking up earlier and working out," and then the morning came and you snoozed your alarm ten times and said, "Eh, maybe tomorrow"? Or have you ever told someone you would call them or hang out with them but then an hour later when you were home on your couch with a bag of Doritos, you just didn't feel like it anymore?

I don't know about you, but I've been there. Many times, I've said things in a moment of emotion, only later to not follow through with my actions. I've also done things in a moment of emotion that I've gone on to regret.

How do these behaviors play out when it comes to relationships and love? If we're honest, there are going to be moments when our feelings will contradict our values or commitments. When you encounter the rush of attraction and love, the giddy talking and looking into each other's eyes, and the singing and dancing together, the emotions of those moments will be *big*. But after a mood swing or an unmet expectation, those feelings change. Emotions make terrible leaders because emotions are inconsistent. They change. They become more or less intense. Even love is more than a fleeting feeling. And the love we desire deep down has less to do with how we feel and more to do with how we serve.

> Emotions make terrible leaders because emotions are inconsistent.

## "I FELL IN LOVE"

You *fell* in love? Like you fell trying to walk in heels? Like me at my senior prom, when I fell down the stairs while the entire student body watched? Why do we describe love, the biggest and most important thing we have on this earth, like it's something we just stumble upon or like it's an accident? If that's how we truly view love, no wonder it keeps running into dead ends. No wonder it continues to fail. No wonder it's full of unfaithfulness and inconsistency.

We are told to follow our heart, so we live with our heart on our sleeve—displaying every emotion or acting on every whim. But if we want a lasting love, we have to know that emotions aren't always trustworthy. So instead of letting our emotions drive every action and decision, we must be led by conviction and wisdom, even if at times that means acting against what our heart wants.

Falling in love is easy. Literally anyone can do it. It's an emotion. You are all caught up in the fantasy. In his book *The New Rules for Love, Sex, and Dating,* Andy Stanley said, "Falling in love is easy; it requires a pulse. Staying in love requires *more.*"[1]

Everyone wants love. Everyone loves love. Or their version of it. That's why television shows and movies and music all center on love. But what most of the world fails to acknowledge is that being in love is more than just an emotion and electricity. It's more than butterflies in your stomach and a romantic kiss. The love that our hearts were designed for is not the kind of love that is based on circumstances or chemistry but the kind of love that says, "No matter what, I will choose you." Love is a choice demonstrated by consistent action.

In the Bible, love is a command. Love God and love people. Not when you feel like it or when the circumstances are just right. Not when you've had adequate sleep or when you're getting what you want. You're to love whether or not it's easy, whether or not it's beneficial to you.

One of my favorite books, *The Sacred Search,* says, "Women, if you simply follow your feelings, you are more likely to fall in love with a guy who will thrill you for twelve to eighteen months as a boyfriend and then frustrate you for five to six decades as a husband."[2] You have to think about what you want ten years down the road. Rich Wilkerson, Jr., said, "Whoever you married is going to be your greatest asset or your greatest liability."[3] Who do you want by your side when everything is going wrong and the infatuation has faded? Who do you want to laugh with? Suffer with? Change the world with? Look for that. Find that. If you want a love that will last, you can't look for a fun, steamy romance.

## DON'T FOLLOW YOUR HEART

When I started dating Grant, we were so infatuated. We felt so strongly for each other, like we were just walking on clouds—nothing could possibly pull us down. We acted like every time we were together, it was a music video. We truly saw ourselves as Troy and Gabriella from *High School Musical*. "You are the music in me!" Every day, I even wore the G necklace he gave me. Our relationship was moving like a freight train. Three weeks in, we were ready to get engaged and run off into the sunset.

It was magnetic, and we just kept falling deeper and deeper for each other. When we saw other couples having issues, we thought, *Aw, poor them. If they only had what we have.* They probably looked at us and thought, *Aw, poor them. They have a rude awakening coming.* And boy, were they right. Anxiety, fear, and insecurity rushed to the surface. Commitment, sacrifice, humility, patience, and communication—gosh, did we have some things to learn!

We were two different people, with two different understandings of love and two different upbringings, in two different seasons of life, all mixed in with long distance. . . . A rude awakening is exactly what happened. As soon as we started feeling these tensions, we began questioning the whole relationship. "Well, maybe you're not who I thought." "Maybe you're just not *the one* anymore." We started bickering and fighting. We were consumed with emotion and letting it dictate our every move, but we wondered why we were unsteady.

That's the problem with being led by your emotions. They are constantly changing. One day I wanted to take his shirt off, and the next day I wanted to bite his head off! That's why you can't always trust your feelings and you can't be led by them.

My focus had to shift from "How do I feel?" to "God, is this your will?" This is a scary and hard prayer to pray. Because your feelings will be telling you *a lot*. One of the hardest things to do is to sacrifice what you feel for what you value most. In the moment, I may feel lazy, selfish, or insecure, but that's not what I value, that's not who I want to be, and that's definitely not God's Spirit inside me. I value serving over being served. I value humility and honor over chemistry and attraction. I value intentionality over convenience.

## WHY FEELINGS ARE VALUABLE

I don't want the takeaway from this chapter to be that feelings are bad and you shouldn't have them. That's the opposite of what I believe. I believe that feelings are created and given by

God and that they are valuable and necessary for you and me to experience all that God has for us, including loving relationships.

There are many reasons I believe feelings are important and valuable.

**Feelings are great indicators.** They tell us where we are experiencing lack and where we are experiencing abundance. We can look at our feelings and know whether our mindset is healthy or not. If we are constantly led by jealousy, fear, insecurity, anxiety, bitterness, comparison, or sadness, undoubtedly something is missing in our lives and we need to look deeper. However, if we are led by joy, peace, patience, kindness, humility, confidence, and contentment, clearly our mindset is healthy and we are experiencing abundance. That is why feelings aren't something we should ignore. We should pay careful attention to them, as they indicate whether our bodies, souls, and spirits are healthy or unhealthy.

**Feelings are great connectors.** Feelings bridge the gap. They help us relate to one another. They make us real. They make us human. When people share hard stories, we can empathize with them because we can feel their pain, and usually we do that by associating their difficulty with things we have felt or experienced in the past. Feelings make relationships what they are, because it is through vulnerability and emotion that we feel seen, heard, understood, affirmed, and needed. Feelings help us connect with other people, with ourselves, and with our faith.

**Feelings are great motivators.** This is why there are TED Talks, motivational movies, and graduation commencement speeches, and this is why coaches give speeches to their players before a big game. Feelings motivate you to get better. It's why the best communicators move you to change by tugging on your emotions. It's why when you watch sad videos of abused or neglected children in impoverished areas, you feel compelled to give or to go serve. Feelings can motivate us to be all that we have the potential to be.

## WHY FEELINGS ARE DANGEROUS

Just as feelings and emotions can be valuable and beautiful, they can also be dangerous and destructive. We have to learn how to manage our emotions and how to listen to and validate them without giving them the reins to make our decisions and lead our life. Feelings—both the good ones and bad ones—can be fleeting and flaky, so it's not wise for us to build our life and destiny on something as inconsistent as our emotions.

Feelings can be bad decision makers. If we always follow whatever our feelings tell us, we could end up down a road of resentment, regret, shame, or even death. Sometimes we may not feel good enough. Sometimes we may feel hopeless. Sometimes we may feel unloved. Sometimes we may feel like ending it all because life is simply too heavy. Just because we may feel those things in the moment doesn't mean they are true and doesn't mean we should act on them.

I grew up hearing the saying "Don't make a permanent decision based on a temporary feeling." Because you can't take it back once it's been done. And often in the heat of the moment, our feelings can be crazy and reckless. Our emotions can make us believe that our circumstances will never change.

> Feelings can be bad decision makers.

Feelings can hurt other people. In the same way that feelings can help you connect and empathize with people, feelings can also cause harm. Think about feelings like jealousy, anger, fear, and sadness. I've learned in my own life that my actions and decisions don't just affect me; they also affect the people around me. Life is so much bigger than just me. Letting my selfish or prideful or lazy feelings lead me could be detrimental to those around me.

I've been on the receiving end of being bullied. Threats were made, actions were taken, rumors were spread, and it was so hurtful. My mom would tell me, "Hurt people hurt people," meaning that because this person was insecure and hurting, she took it out on me. Even though it was so hard to understand at the time how someone could be so mean, I finally understood that it had

> Feelings can hurt other people.

little to do with me and more to do with the other girl's insecurity and hurt.

A lot of us allow our feelings to lead us down some dangerous paths. When we don't feel like loving a particular person, we don't. When we don't feel like fighting for our relationships, we don't. When we feel like saying something out of anger, we say it. When we feel like leaving, we do. When we feel like cheating, we do. When we feel hurt by the other person, we repay them by withholding our love or even hurting them back. These are moments in relationships when feelings can be dangerous and can cost you something you may not want to give up.

## A HEART ON GUARD

What does Madi Prewett Troutt have in common with Steph Curry, Kyrie Irving, and the great Russell Westbrook? At one time in all our lives, we played the point-guard position in basketball. If you're not familiar with the sport, a point guard basically directs the offense for their team. They're usually the best ball handler, keeping the basketball under control and making plays for the team. And they're usually responsible for guarding the other team's point guard.

As a point guard, I was known for being a little aggressive. Okay, I was known for being *a lot* aggressive. I would practice dribbling for hours, run drills with my dad (my coach), and play just as hard whether it was a practice, regular-season game, or post-season game. I took my position seriously. So seriously, in fact, that I was able to be on a team that won four state championships, and I was named MVP twice and all-state honoree three times.

The truth is, I wasn't the best shooter. I was pretty good at dribbling, but my biggest contribution to the team was my ability to guard the other team's point guard. I didn't mess around. One time when I tried to steal the ball, the other point guard, who was much bigger than me, still had it in her hand, but I clung to the ball, refusing to let go. She literally swung the ball from side to side, with me flying back and forth. I didn't let go until the referee blew the whistle. I guarded that ball with my life!

Proverbs 4:23 talks about guarding something else, something much more important than a basketball player: "Above all else, guard your heart, for everything you do flows from it." If our heart affects everything we do—our decisions, our thinking, and our relationships—shouldn't we be protective of it? During most of my years as a point guard, I was good at guarding the ball, but I wasn't that great at guarding my heart—I wasn't diligent about making sure that what was in my heart was trustworthy, good, and true. But just as this verse says, above all else, we should stay on guard when it comes to our heart, because it affects everything we do.

In order to guard our heart, we need it to be characterized by three important things: conviction, wisdom, and discipline.

*A heart of conviction* is led by beliefs, values, and faith. When we have a heart of conviction, our emotions may expire, but our values and beliefs are firm. That's why we should build our lives on our beliefs rather than on our feelings.

Convictions should direct our lives. Our feelings can mask themselves as truth, but when we give in to them and let them lead us, our heart becomes vulnerable, unprotected, unable to discern what's true and what's not. When we are led by convictions, we are led by something stable and steady: our values and beliefs.

*A heart of wisdom* is full of knowledge, insight, vision, and discernment. It knows what's right and what's not. What to say yes to and what to say no to. When to walk away and when to stay. When to speak out and when to be silent.

A heart of wisdom understands that we are three-part beings: spirit, soul (mind and emotions), and body. The part that you feed and give the most attention will be the strongest and assume control. Your spirit is led by convictions, your soul is led by emotions, and your body is led by cravings. A heart of wisdom knows that the spirit should be fed the most, for it should always be in the driver's seat.

*A heart of discipline* chooses self-control, creates boundaries for protection, and knows its priorities. A heart of discipline says, "I choose you," even when it's hard. Because true love isn't based on something that could change overnight. According to God, true love never fails (1 Corinthians 13:8). How can love never fail? It must mean that it's more than a lustful attraction or sappy emotion. It's a sacrifice. A commitment. A choice.

Instead of wearing our heart on our sleeve, let's reframe our thinking and guard our heart. A heart on guard is careful, uses wisdom, and is led by conviction. Love can be an emotion, an intense emotion, but the right kind of love, the love we all deeply desire, is much more than that.

> The heart is deceitful above all things,
> and beyond cure.
> Who can understand it?
>
> —Jeremiah 17:9

## BONUS CONTENT

Using your smartphone,
scan the code for bonus content.

waterbrookmultnomah.com/the-love
-everybody-wants-chapter-7-bonus-content

# 8

## SHAME ON YOU

### Break Up with Shame

> *Can I really be forgiven for what I've done?*
> *How can I escape these feelings of shame?*
> *How do I not let the pain of my past hinder my future?*

The whole eighth grade saw my butt.

Before I explain, let me ask, Have you ever been traumatized by an embarrassing moment? Well, this was mine.

I got invited to a pool party and was so excited. I was feeling pretty good about myself and my brand-new polka-dot string bikini. Of course, all my girlfriends were starting to develop shapely bodies. I, on the other hand, still looked like a fifth-grade boy—flat as a board!

When I got to the pool party, I pulled out my camera so I could take some cute pictures before my hair got all wet and gross. I grabbed my best friend, and we stood side by side on the edge of the pool and counted to three to capture the standard jump-in-the-pool-holding-hands picture. As we started to jump, my friend went too early. Instead of grabbing my hand, she accidentally grabbed my swimsuit bottom string. When she jumped, she took my bottoms with her, as that string was the only thing keeping those suckers up. I looked around, and the entire eighth grade was pointing at me and laughing and making jokes. Not knowing what else to do, I jumped in as fast as I could. I grabbed my bottoms and quickly tied them back up.

I got out of the pool, beyond embarrassed. I couldn't believe that happened! My face was burning red. I ran to get my phone, acting like my mom was calling me and telling me I had to come home. This was the talk of school for the next few weeks, and I decided that day that I would never wear a string bikini again.

I feel like I have more than my fair share of embarrassing stories. Like the time I was walking around the grocery store and a girl came up to me and informed me that my dress was tucked into my underwear. I was mortified. I had been walking around like that for almost an hour! Every so often, these moments pop up in my memory. When I think back to embarrassing moments, I can still feel the burning in my cheeks and the pit in my stomach. I feel ashamed.

So, back to you. Do you ever reflect on moments from the past and feel like you want to die of embarrassment? Have you ever done something so weird to get a guy's attention? Or have you ever walked out of the bathroom with toilet paper stuck to your shoe?

Wherever your past actions fall on the shame spectrum—

from prank calling someone to find out if he liked you back, to making out with a random guy because it felt good in the moment, to doing even more with your boyfriend—these missteps and mistakes can't take away your promised future. Shame can't steal the ever-present reality that you are loved and made for a purpose.

So, wherever you find yourself today—whatever you have done, whatever has happened to you, or whatever has been done to you—it's time to shake off that shame. As long as you're holding on to that feeling, you can't experience the fullness of relationships the way God intended for you. I want to take the time to unearth the shame we keep hidden and bring it to light. Because only then can true freedom be found.

Lisa Bevere said it like this: "The battle is not against who we have been, it is all out war against who we are becoming."[1] Shame shackles us to who we were and what we did—to those moments that make us cringe with regret. But our effort to change our past is wasted. Conversely, our effort to become who God wants us to be is *required* to receive his best for our lives.

## WHAT IS SHAME?

When I was twenty-one, I accidentally left a voicemail for my boss instead of my boyfriend. I was driving and typed in the first letter of my boyfriend's name, and without even paying attention, I clicked on the first name that popped up and called. He didn't answer, so I left a voicemail. In the voicemail

I talked in a baby voice, telling him he was cute and I missed him, and then I hung up and continued to go on about my day.

I went straight into biology, and after the class ended, I noticed a text from my boss. I opened the message, and it said, "I assume you didn't mean to leave that voicemail for me." I panicked and looked at my recent calls. My boss's name was at the top of the list. I had an instant feeling of dread in the pit of my stomach. I was so ashamed, I wanted to crawl into a hole.

Later that day, I apologized to him and called his wife and explained to her that the voicemail was meant for my boyfriend and not her husband. I felt so much shame, even though it was a complete accident. I started to feel different around my boss and the whole team, and I began to isolate myself, hiding from everyone because of my silly mistake.

Now, the situation of me calling my boss instead of my boyfriend is small compared with what many of you are carrying today. Many of you are battling a deeper shame that consumes and paralyzes. It makes you want to run away. You feel the need to cover up. Feeling shame can lead to hiding, lying, isolating, escaping, numbing, avoiding, or even dying. Shame goes much deeper than many realize. It makes things personal. Shame attacks your identity and self-worth.

Three friends of mine who have battled shame because of things that they have done or that have been done to them have bravely and freely given me permission to share their stories in the hope of bringing freedom and courage to you.

*Shame attacks your identity and self-worth.*

The first girl we will call Chloe. She grew up in a Christian home with an amazing family. She was always known as a goody-goody her whole life—until college. She joined a sorority and started hanging out with friends who loved to party. It didn't take her long to join in, drinking and hooking up with guys, compromising her own standards and beliefs. Partying became the norm for her every weekend.

After one night of particularly heavy drinking with friends, Chloe, her best friend, and the two guys they were with went back to her apartment to hang out. "Hanging out" turned into making out, with each girl and her respective guy going into separate rooms. In the morning, Chloe was awakened by her friend, who was freaking out, saying that a video was circulating of Chloe doing sexual things to the guy she was with the night before.

Apparently, some guy had walked in on them and videoed without them knowing. That video was put on social media and sent in a group chat to the whole baseball team, which happened to have some players who had attended her high school. She worried that people from her hometown—especially her Christian, conservative family and friends—would hear about it or see it and be disappointed in her. She was so ashamed.

Shame led to depression, which resulted in her isolating herself from her family and close friends. Chloe battled suicidal thoughts, thinking she could never escape the embarrassment and shame. Not only did she feel cut off from friends and family, but she also felt God could never love her and forgive her for what she had done.

The second girl we will call Olivia. She also grew up in a Christian household and had prided herself in being the "good Christian virgin girl."

The night of her high school graduation, every virtue she held so tightly came crashing down. Her church's youth group had decided to celebrate graduation by playing pickleball. A guy she had a crush on was there, and they flirted most of the night. Once pickleball ended and it was time to say goodbye, he continued to flirt with her and led her into his car. Next thing she knew, they were kissing in the back seat of his car. But what she hoped was just innocent fun quickly turned aggressive. He held her down and undressed her against her will. Olivia's body went limp, and a tear streamed down her face as her virginity was stolen in less than two minutes. She just kept saying, "This is not how this is supposed to go."

When Olivia later turned to the church for prayer and healing, the pastor suggested she had been leading guys on and *her actions* were the reason the assault happened. Not only did the act itself create shame, but the rejection that followed compounded it. She felt defiled, dirty, and exposed. And as the pastor's words continued to ring in her mind, she began to believe she really was the one to blame. She couldn't even look at herself in the mirror. Shame quickly turned to anger, then numbness.

Feeling like a failure, Olivia gave up on purity completely. She turned to pornography and other relationships, hoping to silence the pain for a moment, but those things only led to deeper shame. She told herself she was fine and didn't care.

But inside she truly felt dirty and hopeless, thinking, *How could anyone love me after the choices I have made?*

The third girl we will call Phoebe. She grew up in a family that never showed the value of loving God and loving people. She didn't know self-worth, so, from a young age, she looked to boys to fill that void. She wanted them to make her feel worthy, even if it meant she had to give a piece of herself to them.

She got into a toxic relationship that stole everything from her—every bit of confidence, self-respect, or hope she had. The guy only cared about what she could give him physically, and she wondered if maybe that was the only way to love. She finally ended that relationship but continued to put herself in toxic situations and crave validation from guys because, in her mind, it meant that someone finally wanted her. Phoebe then reached a point that a guy's attention wasn't enough. So she turned to a girl and got romantically involved, which only created more confusion.

Desperate for any form of love and belonging, Phoebe's identity was tied to her relationships and whether her partners made her feel like she was "enough." As a result, she was depressed and anxious all the time and felt immense shame for giving away her purity.

But, eventually, all three girls found hope.

Chloe had been trapped in depression and isolation for almost a year when a friend invited her to join her small group at church. She did and it ultimately changed her life. She realized that God had forgiven her and that she didn't have to carry shame anymore. She is not proud of her earlier choices, but she is thankful that she found freedom and hope. Chloe now helps other women who are bound in shame find the freedom they were made for.

Olivia had a different experience. Halfway through her college freshman year, she was awakened in the middle of the night, sensing God in a way she never had before. She felt him say, "It's time you choose . . . me or the world."

For so long, she had been running to other things and other people to give her what only God could. And in that moment, she decided it was time to go all in with God and let him have every piece of her life. She said, "This journey has not been easy, but it has been real, vulnerable, freeing, and redeeming. There is not one part of my story I want erased or edited anymore. For God has turned my pain into my purpose and my shame into joy!" She said that Isaiah 61:7 is her anthem: "Instead of your shame, you will receive a double portion . . . and everlasting joy will be yours."

In Phoebe's case, she had struggled to accept that God still loved her and thought of her as worthy. She felt that no true Christian man would ever be able to love her because of her past. But after years of believing the lies of the Enemy and settling for a life that was less than God's best, she was asked to be a part of a freedom group her church offered. There, she heard and felt God's truth clearer than ever. She surrendered her heart to God again and he redeemed her. She confessed to those in her group, and they prayed for her, allowing her to feel freedom and hope.

For the first time in her whole life, Phoebe felt she was worthy because God was worthy. She accepted that she is a daughter of God, fearfully and wonderfully made. God began to wipe away her shame and disgrace, and in him she found all that her heart had been searching for: a love that never fails.

I'm not going to pretend that any of their lives instantly or magically became easier, or that their memories of trauma vanished. But as they each understood and received forgiveness and grace from Jesus and pursued godly community with confession and prayer, the stronghold that shame had on them loosened and continued to lose its power over time.

So, what exactly is shame? One of my favorite speakers and authors, Lysa TerKeurst, had a guest on her podcast, therapist Jim Cress, and he described SHAME as an acronym that stands for "self-hatred at my expense."[2] I thought that was so powerful, and it sums up exactly what shame is and what it will do if we let it. Chances are, we all have been plagued by this deadly disease, and we are the ones paying the price. Not only does shame kill our relationship with ourselves; it also kills our relationships with others.

> Not only does shame kill our relationship with ourselves; it also kills our relationships with others.

If we believe that we can't be loved, we will find it impossible to be in a healthy and loving relationship with anyone else. We will distance ourselves from others to protect ourselves from being fully known. If we find ourselves thinking, *If you really knew me, you wouldn't want to be in a relationship with me,* this is a prime indicator that shame is controlling our lives.

Shame says, "Because of what I have done . . ." or "Because of what has been done to me . . ."

"I don't feel good enough."

"No one wants to date me; something must be wrong
    with me."

"Relationships never work out for me. I must be the
    problem."

"Nothing good will ever happen to me."

"I don't deserve to be in a loving relationship."

"It would be better if I weren't here."

When we are overwhelmed with shame, we will believe these lies: *It will always be this way. I deserve it.* Shame is always pointing the finger at someone (usually ourselves). Shame makes us believe we are the problem, leading us to question our worth, identity, and purpose.

> Shame makes us believe we are the problem, leading us to question our worth, identity, and purpose.

## THE CYCLE OF SHAME

All cycles work the same way. One step leads to another step, which leads to another and another. Once you're in a cycle, it can be difficult to get out of it. And most of the time, you don't even realize you're in one until you're repeating the steps again and again and again. This is especially true of the shame cycle. That's why it's important to recognize each step so you can be self-aware and take immediate action. Because time spent in any harmful cycle is time you can't get back.

Brené Brown is a researcher, professor, author, lecturer,

and podcast host (I mean, she really does it all) who has spent decades studying topics like vulnerability, courage, and shame.[3] Based on Brown's findings and my own experiences, here are the typical steps of the shame cycle:

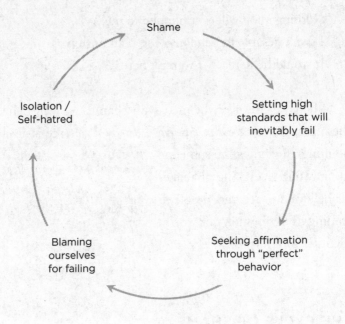

Shame

Setting high standards that will inevitably fail

Seeking affirmation through "perfect" behavior

Blaming ourselves for failing

Isolation / Self-hatred

Shame can also wreak havoc on our thought lives—and as a result, it leaks into *all* areas of our lives. Shame-based thinking can lead to . . .

- **The pressure to perform.** We try to prove our worthiness or belonging. We think, *I can get rid of this shame if I can just be perfect and give a perfect performance.* Because we think our worth is derived from the things we do, we set insanely high standards for ourselves, which we will inevitably fail to reach.

- **Criticizing ourselves and others.** When our standards aren't met and we aren't perfect, we blame ourselves or others. I grew up hearing, "Hurt people hurt people"—which is true. But I would even take it further to say, "Shamed people shame people." Usually when we do this, it results less from thinking and more from reacting. We are so miserable in our own shame that we can't help but throw that onto others.

- **Isolation.** We think, *If I'm the problem, it's better for everyone if I just disappear.* This can result in running away or hiding, if not literally, then emotionally. Either we run away from people and our problems, or we try to hide and cover up our problems.

- **Self-defeating thoughts and self-hatred.** This is when it can get dangerous. We can hate ourselves and our lives. We begin to lower our expectations so we don't get disappointed. We think, *Everything I touch will ultimately fail, and I will be let down, so it's easier to not hope.*

- **Victimization.** Shame can even cause us to play victim. We blame others by shifting responsibility from ourselves to others. This leads to every day being a pity party. Believe me—this isn't the kind of party you want to be at, friend.

## SHAME VERSUS GUILT

Shame isn't just guilt, embarrassment, or conviction. It is much deeper and deadlier. Brené Brown explained it this way: "Shame is a focus on self. Guilt is a focus on behavior. Shame is 'I am bad.' Guilt is 'I did something bad.'"[4] She also said that shame is "the intensely painful feeling or experience of believing that we are flawed and therefore unworthy of love and belonging—something we've experienced, done, or failed to do makes us unworthy of connection."[5] With guilt, we can always get a fresh start. With shame, we are caught in a never-ending black hole, because the problem stays with us. In fact, with shame, we are the problem.

Guilt is about disobeying a law or standard, but shame is about how I think others see me or how I see myself. Guilt is getting a speeding ticket and thinking, *Well, that was irresponsible. I'll do better next time.* Shame is getting that same ticket and thinking, *I'm a horrible person because I was speeding—what was I thinking? I can't do anything right!*

Guilt can be a beautiful step to repentance, forgiveness, and freedom. Guilt is your conscience telling you that you are better than that! But let guilt fester too long, and it can move into shame. When you feel healthy guilt, acknowledge your wrong, repent, make amends if needed, and adjust. Then move on.

## SHAME VERSUS EMBARRASSMENT

Embarrassment is also different from shame. Embarrassment usually follows doing something stupid in front of others and then caring what they think, like losing my bikini bottoms at a pool party or being the center of attention and disliking it. Embarrassment often happens in the moment and doesn't linger for long. It usually results in turning red in the face or hiding for a moment. Embarrassment is very different from shame in that it is momentary and action based. It rarely causes one to question their identity or purpose or live any differently than before the embarrassing moment.

We all get embarrassed every now and then. Embarrassment shows that we're human and demonstrates a certain level of self-awareness. When we can learn to embrace our imperfections, embarrassing moments become something we can laugh about and shrug off. Life is too short to take every stumble seriously! We have to realize that sometimes we're going to make silly mistakes—wear a see-through dress, trip in front of a crowd, or have spinach in our teeth on a date. Learning how to quickly move past these cringeworthy moments is how we keep embarrassment from turning into shame.

## SHAME VERSUS CONVICTION

A different feeling we sometimes have can feel like shame: conviction. Although conviction is often mistaken for guilt or condemnation, it couldn't be further from it. *Conviction* is defined as "a firmly held belief or opinion."[6] Conviction leads to a strong belief system and choices that point to those beliefs. It's what we should be striving for. Conviction gives you courage to stand up for what you believe in, grace to walk in those beliefs, and strength to hold firm to those beliefs no matter what others say or do. Shame causes you to doubt your identity, beliefs, values, and purpose. Conviction gives you the ability to stay true to those very things.

> *Conviction calls you higher. Shame drags you down.*

In the book *Love Changes Everything*, Micah Berteau explained that conviction calls you higher and reminds you of who you are, whereas shame drags you down and reminds you of your sin.[7]

I want to be led by conviction in my decisions, thoughts, and actions. When people think about me, I hope they say that I am a woman of conviction. In fact, I pray we are all led by a spirit of conviction in our day-to-day lives. Not obsessed with what others think of us. Not changing who we are for others to accept us. Not compromising what we believe so that we will be more likable. Not caving to the pressures around us. Let's stand firm in conviction—knowing who we are and what we believe.

As we've seen, shame isn't guilt. Shame isn't embarrassment. Shame isn't conviction. Shame is believing that we are beyond the reach of grace and forgiveness. Shame lowers our view of ourselves. It says, "I'm bad because I did something bad." Shame is when we allow our darkest moments and biggest missteps to define us. Our mistakes become our identity, so we hide, isolate, and detach. Shame is dangerous. Why? It strips us of the power to change, because we begin to believe we aren't capable of being any better than our sin. Shame in relationships can be dangerous; it can create unhealthiness and toxic tendencies like blaming, isolating, lying, manipulating, and hiding. It's impossible to have a healthy or lasting love if one or both persons are operating from a place of shame.

I want us to take the steps to remove the barrier of shame from our lives. Because shame-based thinking isn't from God, and it will keep you from all he has for you. The way to get rid of shame is to see yourself how God sees you and to receive the forgiveness he extends.

## SHAME ENDS HERE

One of my favorite sayings is "Where shame ends, grace begins." Shame tells us that we will never be enough and we are stuck in our sins, mistakes, and problems. Grace meets us at the door of our insecurity and pain, and invites us to be free. Grace agrees that we are weak and sinful, but it leads us to the truth, and the truth sets us free.

How can we fight against shame? Here are some helpful ways.

### Shame Loses Power in a Relationship with Jesus

Not that these are listed in any particular order, but *this* is the most important step in our fight against shame. A relationship with Jesus by faith helps to heal us of shame, bringing freedom. As Christians, we know that we have been healed, set free, and made new. We know that our freedom isn't based on what we have or haven't done nor on what we can or can't do; it's based on the finished work of Jesus Christ. This means that no matter how dirty and messy and broken we have been, Jesus can make us clean and worthy. Part of Jesus's mission on earth was to release captives from their prisons (Luke 4:18)— and what a prison shame can be. That's not to say that once we're in a relationship with Jesus, shame doesn't try to creep back in. It does! That's why it's critical to test our thoughts by running them through the filter of what God says is true—that we are forgiven, chosen, and loved, no matter what.

## Shame Loses Power in the Right Community

Another powerful way to fight shame is to be fully known and to know others fully. When we share with others the ways that shame has threatened to hold us hostage—and we're met with empathy—shame fades away. It loses the power of isolation and fear. There is healing in confession!

Dealing with shame is one of the hardest things. You want to run and hide. You don't want to show your face. You feel like such a screwup. And to make it worse, you feel all alone. But as soon as you share with someone and they encourage you and affirm that you aren't alone and they have been through similar things, you start to feel better. You feel hope again. You feel like you can come out from under your shell. No need to hide anymore, because someone else gets it!

I have seen in my own life, and for those that have shared their shame with me, freedom did come. Not overnight and not easily, but healing began when they received forgiveness from Jesus and confessed to community. When we confront our shame and bring our sin and struggles into the light, we make room for healing and freedom!

## Shame Loses Power When We Are Quick to Forgive and Repent

We are called to extend grace not judgment—not only to others but also to ourselves. You have been forgiven; now you are called to forgive. Matthew 6:14 says, "If you forgive other people when they sin against you, your heavenly Father will also forgive you." I believe God gives us this command because he knows the power of forgiveness, not just received but also given.

One of the things I have learned in life, especially now in marriage, is the freedom that comes with being quick to forgive. I feel like it comes much easier to my husband, Grant, than it does to me. We even have a competition now to see who can be the first to forgive. Repentance and forgiveness break down the walls of hostility, shame, fear, and anger.

Repentance is realizing sin and choosing a new way of loving others and God. It's turning away from sin and turning toward God. When we repent, we are redeemed through the blood of Jesus, the forgiveness of our sins. But forgiveness is something we are not only offered but called to.

To get the love we all want, we have to *learn* from our past shame but not stay stuck in it. "Shame on you" will always hurt you, hold you back, and lead to more shame. Move forward knowing that you are so much more than the sum of your darkest moments—you are *God's*. Shame may have held you prisoner before, but not anymore.

> Move forward knowing that you are so much more than the sum of your darkest moments—you are God's.

Sometimes we bolt because we hate to repent. It feels like death to confess. But when God calls us to something that feels backward, it is usually his path to our freedom. The path out of shame is to see our sin and turn from it toward our God.

—Jennie Allen, *Anything*

## BONUS CONTENT

Using your smartphone,
scan the code for bonus content.

waterbrookmultnomah.com/the-love
-everybody-wants-chapter-8-bonus-content

# 9

## thank u, next

### Healing from Rejection

> *What was the point of that failed relationship?*
> *Why did God allow that rejection to happen?*
> *How do I not live in fear that I will be rejected again?*

Do you remember the trust fall—where you stand in front of another person with your back facing them? You count to three and then just fall back, and the other person's job is to catch you. I never could do it. All my friends would do it for fun. "Okay, my turn! Catch me!" I didn't understand what was so fun about leaving your fate in the hands of someone else. Okay, *fate* is a strong word. But still, I didn't trust them to catch me. What if they moved and let me fall? What if they fell with me? No way! So, I would sit back and watch as they so carelessly fell back into the arms of another friend.

To this day, even with people I trust with all my heart, I can't do the trust fall. I will turn around and look before I fall back, or I will step back to catch myself. I don't know what it is in me. The worst thing that could happen is I fall, and why is that so bad? But for whatever reason, it freaks me out.

Because my greatest fear is getting betrayed—getting rejected. I would always think, *They are going to drop me. They are going to let me fall. Then they will point and laugh at me.* In a way, it revealed to me that what was going on in my head and heart went much deeper than just a game. In everyday, real life, I was always ready to catch myself, always ready for defense, always in protection mode, just in case someone betrayed me.

One day, I was talking to my therapist about this, and she looked at me and said, "Madi, you have to learn to change the narrative in your head, or it is going to cost you the love you could have." I sat on it for a while and thought to myself, *She's right.* It's impossible to fully love and fully live if you are afraid of the fall. We have to learn to trust. We have to learn to let our walls down. And that's hard to do when you've experienced rejection and heartbreaking relationships. So, if you've experienced that, I get it. It's hard to recover and survive, let alone thrive and let someone else in.

> *It's impossible to fully love and fully live if you are afraid of the fall.*

## REJECTION IS REDIRECTION

I'm a dreamer. I love to think of big goals for my future, set high expectations for what I want and what I think I'm capable of, and envision all those things coming to pass exactly as I planned. Even in my mid-twenties, I can already laugh when I think about everything I thought I'd have by now in life. I can't even count the number of times I've been rerouted. I've tried to grasp at control of every part of my life. Yet the more I tried to grasp and the tighter I clenched my hands, the more everything seemed to fall apart.

It's tempting to let redirections disorient and disappoint us. Maybe you think, *But, Madi, I really am upset that my life isn't looking like I thought it would.* And I will be the first to tell you on a deep level, *I feel you.* I've walked through those same emotions, as all my hopes for love and plans for the future have come crashing down more times than I can count.

But the more I learn to stop holding on so tightly to my plans and wants, and the more I learn to trust God, the more evident it becomes that it is God—and God alone—leading my life. His ways are perfect and always better than my own. When God ordains something, you can't stop it. When it's not God, it will stop itself. Acts 5:38–39 tells us, "If their purpose or activity is of human origin, it will fail. But if it is from God, you will not be able to stop these men; you will only find yourselves fighting against God." In other words, *if it's not God, it will fail; if it is God, it will prevail.*

The same thing can be said about our lives. We often think we know what is best, so we get in the driver's seat of life and set out for our destination. Then we make a few wrong turns and ultimately end up somewhere we didn't expect to be. Usually, this place is filled with depression, anxiety, regret, shame, brokenness, and loneliness.

Oftentimes, we just go about our lives and our relationships without even taking a second to ask ourselves, *Is this God's way? Is this God's best? Am I walking in God's will?* So, how can we get to that place? In other words, how do we do life and relationships God's way? What is God's will? How can we really trust that God knows what we need and want?

## THE PURPOSE OF REJECTION

I know about rejection a little too well! Getting cheated on by my first love, not getting picked by the sororities I wanted, friends betraying me and letting me down. I'm sure you have your own stories of rejection too. You might also be familiar with another rejection I experienced . . . because it aired on national TV on *The Bachelor*.

You wanna know what's worse than getting rejected? Getting rejected in front of millions of people. Here's what it *felt* like: "Madi, you're good, but you're not great. You're worth dating, but you're not worth settling down for." I felt momentarily guilty for having standards for my future spouse. *I'll never find the love I want,* I thought. *Because I'm obviously not worthy of it.*

Rejection has a way of making us feel small and undeserving. And as much as I hate rejection, I've learned that, in this broken and sinful world, it is inevitable. Yet I've also had to learn over the years how to praise God for the closed doors, failed relationships, broken dreams, unmet expectations, and nos. Of course, I don't jump up and down and cheer when I get cheated on, or when someone else is picked instead of me, or when I lose the job, or when I feel left out in some way. Those moments bring so much hurt.

One thing is for sure: God's redirection will always require us to let go of our expectations and plans. We will have to surrender and trust.

Trusting others is something I'm bad at, if I'm being honest. Maybe the same is true for you. Maybe, over the years of unmet expectations, rejections, losses, and betrayals, we've all developed some trust issues.

Many of us translate our trust issues with other people to our relationship with God. We think, *No one can be trusted. Even if they mean well, they could still reject me.* That's completely true—of humans. But God is perfect. His love for us is infallible. Never once in the history of humankind has God rejected one of his own children. He's not going to start with you or me. But still, we so often use the same reasoning when it comes to trusting people *and* when it comes to trusting God.

I think many of us just don't *understand* trust. We think trust is contingent on circumstances. We tell ourselves that when things change or when that person changes, we will be happy. When our circumstances take a turn for the good, we will be content and believe that God really does have our best in mind. As long as our goals and expectations are being met, we trust God with what happens next. But that is conditional trust. Are you secure enough to accept God's answers even if they aren't what you want to hear or expect to hear?

For me, rejection initiated a panic sequence that sent me spiraling. *This isn't what I expected. This isn't what I wanted. This isn't what I planned for.* The problem with my thought patterns

> God's redirection will always expose what matters to us most.

was that they all centered around one person: Madi. My fear in the face of disappointment was a reflection of what was in my heart. God's redirection will always expose what matters to us most. Feeling disappointment isn't always wrong, but it does show where we've placed our hope.

God's redirection forces something out of our hands that we had hoped to keep. Through that, we begin to realize God's plan for our lives doesn't equate to the easy or comfortable road. Rather, he is working all things, even this disappointment, for our good—as Romans 8:28 reminds us: "We know that in all things God works for the good of those who love him, who have been called according to his purpose."

## REJECTION IS PROTECTION

"I said no!" Many of us grew up hearing these words, whether from parents, teachers, grandparents, or babysitters. We recognize at a young age that these words are what keep us from all we want and think we deserve.

For me as a kid, a no felt hard to understand. I couldn't understand why I couldn't run into the ocean without my floaties or why I couldn't have candy and chips for every meal. I didn't understand why everything was childproof: the windows, the doors, the outlets, the drawers. In the moment, I would cry in frustration because I felt like my parents were keeping me from all the fun I could be having. As I got older, no meant I couldn't hang around certain friends or go to the parties all my friends were going to.

Sometimes a no feels unfair, like we're being made to miss out. Sometimes it feels like rejection and it's hurtful. We get angry at our parents, lashing out: "This is so unfair! You must not love me enough! Carly's parents let her go! They are way cooler than you!" I had many moments like this, but as I got older, I began to understand that my parents' no was not from a lack of love or care but rather from an abundance of deep love and care. They would rather dissatisfy me for a moment than watch me do something I would regret for the rest of my life. Their no wasn't rejection; it was protection. They were protecting my heart, my character, my purpose, and my safety. I couldn't see it at the time, but I am who I am, and I am where I am, because they saw something I couldn't. They protected me from what I thought I wanted, because they knew what I needed. God does the same thing with us. We don't always understand it in the moment, and it can oftentimes be painful, but we must trust that if God gives us a no, it's for our betterment.

Once, I lay in my mom's lap, crying because I felt rejected by my friends. They all made plans and didn't include me, then proceeded to tell me they didn't want to be my friends anymore. I couldn't understand why at the time, and it felt like the end of the world. My mom wiped my tears, tucked my hair behind my ears, and told me, "Sometimes you gain the most by losing what you thought was best." She was always right, even if I didn't like to admit it.

> *Sometimes you gain the most by losing what you thought was best.*

## A BETTER WAY

When I got engaged to Grant, everyone kept asking me how I was feeling. I would respond with honesty: "I've found the best yes—the person God has set apart just for me. Yes, it took a lot longer than I thought it would. Yes, it looks different than I thought it would. But I've never been more confident in God's will for my life."

What I meant by that response is that I had to realign many of my goals and expectations. For example, I *expected* to be married at twenty-two to a pastor. I *expected* to have kids by twenty-six. When that didn't work out, I vowed to never marry a pastor. I then met Grant and knew from our first date that he was the one. We talked about dreams and aspirations. Months later, Grant felt led to be a pastor and go into full-time ministry. Oh, the irony! I *expected* that when I found my person, it would be easy and dreamy. Our relationship was full of highs and lows, twists and turns. Yet there was also a pervasive peace. I *expected* to get engaged in three months. We waited eight months (I know that's still quick, but it's long when you are pursuing purity!). I *expected* the engagement season to be perfect and feel like a romantic movie. There were some tears, a lot of stress, and really hard moments.

My expectations weren't always met, things didn't always go according to plan, and my prayers didn't all get answered. Yet I'm so thankful that God didn't answer all my prayers the way I wanted him to. He had *better* plans for my life than I did. He had a better yes. He had a better way. Grant is everything

I prayed for. He is exactly what I need, and his character and heart have exceeded all my expectations. The year 2022 was when I was supposed to get married. Not 2018, like I thought. God was in every detail, refining, building, and preparing. It wasn't always easy, but it was God. And he is better, and his ways are greater.

Remember how I said earlier that the trust fall was one of my greatest fears? I couldn't seem to do it with my family or friends. When it came to trusting someone else and letting go of control, I hesitated and grew fearful. One day, Grant looked at me and said, "We're doing the trust fall."

I looked at him with big eyes and said, "You know I can't!" He insisted and I continued to resist.

He finally said, "If you don't do this trust fall, you are communicating that you don't fully trust me."

I knew in that moment I had a decision to make. So, I stood in front of him, let out a big sigh, and said, "Okay, you got me?"

He assured me, "Madi, I'm not going anywhere." When I fell back into his arms, I felt indescribable relief, joy, and freedom. This probably sounds a little cheesy or silly to you, but it was big for me. I had found the one I was willing to trust to catch me, and I was reminded of how many times God has stood behind me saying, "Madi, you can trust me. Let go of control. Fall back. I'm not going anywhere."

Instead of seeing that guy who walked away as a curse, see the situation as a blessing. Maybe, just maybe, what you see and feel as a disappointment is just the setup for the greatness that awaits you. It may look different from what you expected,

> That closed door is God's way of telling you that there is better than what you just tried to settle for.

but it'll be better than you ever imagined. That closed door is God's way of telling you that there is better than what you just tried to settle for.

> One taught me love
> One taught me patience
> And one taught me pain. . . .

The one and only Ariana Grande sang these words in her song "thank u, next."[1] Even though I don't stand by every word in the song or even the message she intended to send with it, I do think we can take away an important message from the lyrics above.

Grande expressed gratitude to her exes. I want us to think, feel, and say, "I am so grateful for my ex. I am so grateful for that closed door. I am so grateful for that no." I want us to be able to say thank you for those moments of rejection. I don't mean in a sassy or sarcastic, revenge-seeking kind of way. I mean with a heart of gratitude for all that the rejections have taught us.

Discover how to trust that God does everything—even saying no—out of goodness and love. No longer will we let rejections break us; instead, we will let them shape us, teach us, and propel us into our God-given destiny. We know who we are. We trust in the God that created us. So, we look those rejections in the face, and we say, "Thank you, next."

Rejection is merely a redirection; a course correction to your destiny.

—BRYANT MCGILL, *Simple Reminders*

## BONUS CONTENT

Using your smartphone,
scan the code for bonus content.

waterbrookmultnomah.com/the-love
-everybody-wants-chapter-9-bonus-content

# 10

## SINGLE AS A PRINGLE

### More Than Surviving Singleness

> *Why me?*
> *How can finding love be so easy for everyone else?*
> *Why am I the only single person I know?*

Being single can make you wonder, *Why me?* and *How can finding love be so easy for everyone else?* It can cause you to question if there is something wrong with you. We often feel that we are not enough while in our single state.

> *We often feel that we are not enough while in our single state.*

Have you heard the phrase "single as a dollar bill"? I'm not a fan of it, because who wants a single dollar? Nor do I love the phrase "single as a Pringle." Who wants just one Pringle? I know for me, when I eat my Pringles or my Oreos, I eat them in bulk. Just one Pringle feels insufficient. How tempting to view our own state of singleness in the same way: Insufficient. Lonely. It can even be depressing. We need another dollar or another Pringle or another human to feel complete and secure. Yet this isn't how we are meant to view our seasons of singleness.

But I sure understand the feeling. I'm the girl who cringed every time my great-grandmother, Mawmaw, asked me on the phone, "Have you found a boyfriend yet?" She was in her mid-nineties, so I think she would forget she had just asked me that same question the week before, or maybe she thought her constant pressing would lead to me finding a boyfriend.

At first I would get so irritated when she asked. "No, Mawmaw. I am still single."

And I would hear a sigh on the other end of the line. "Ahh. Well. That's okay. You'll find someone . . ."

*Okay, Mawmaw, I get it!* In time, I was able to laugh and remind her, "I am genuinely content and happy with where I am in my life!"

But I've also had many seasons of singleness that felt long and incredibly hard. I had to learn to celebrate everyone else in their seasons of highs and happiness while I was in my season of loneliness and longing. Singleness didn't feel like a gift; it felt more like the leftovers in the fridge that no one wanted. But in this chapter, I want us to learn together how we can view singleness as a blessing and opportunity, how we can find contentment and wholeness in whatever season we are in, and how we can choose to let go and trust God's best—even if it's not what we thought it would look like.

## I'M SO GLAD I'M SINGLE!

One time I was having lunch with my mentor, and she looked at me and said, "You should be so glad you are single. What a gift!"

That idea created uneasiness in the pit of my stomach. Why would I be glad or grateful for such a season? My twenty-two-year-old mind couldn't comprehend. How could she say that when she had been married for fifteen years and had her perfect family? I felt like responding, "Well, I don't agree! This is a gift I would like to exchange, thank you. I think the gift of marriage is a much better fit for me."

As I grow older, I see exactly what she meant, and it's true. I started to believe it as a single. Even now, married, I still believe it. I started writing this book when I was single, and I wrote almost this entire chapter before I even met Grant! Singleness truly is a gift. Not only is it a gift, but singleness is also the *most* crucial season of your life, because who you are here will determine who you will be there.

> Singleness is the most crucial season of your life, because who you are here will determine who you will be there.

Singleness allowed me to grow in my faith. Singleness gave me the opportunity to travel the world and be adventurous. It was a time I could fully devote to my friends and family, finding community and doing life with people who made me better. A time I could learn all about myself: what I liked, my weaknesses, my strengths, and so much more. I could focus on becoming the best version of me.

## THE THREE H'S FOR YOUR SEASON OF SINGLENESS

I'd like to share the three greatest gifts singleness gave me—what I call the three H's—and hopefully they encourage and challenge you.

### 1. Holiness

Singleness allows you to truly become complete in Christ—to discover who you are and what your purpose is. Until Jesus comes first in your life, you will place unrealistic expectations on others and consistently be let down. A lot of times, we allow other people to shape our relationship with God and ourselves. Although those around us should encourage us in our faith and confidence, they can't be our foundation. Singleness gives you the time and opportunity to get your heart right before God and become confident in who he is and who he has called you to be—holy.

Holiness may sound like a daunting calling, but it's one issued to us if we agree to follow Christ. What does *holy* even mean? A simple definition I've heard is that to be holy means to be set apart for a specific purpose. The Bible tells believers that we should be holy because Jesus is holy (1 Peter 1:16). That doesn't mean we're without sin (that's impossible), but it does mean we have a unique purpose—to glorify God with our lives.

In other words, if we say we're Christians (Christ-followers), there's something different about the choices we make, the words we say, and the way we live, because we answer to the authority of Jesus and not society. If we want to be holy—to be set apart—we view our lives as fulfilling a calling, not fulfilling ourselves.

We might practice holiness by dressing modestly, holding boundaries in physical intimacy, avoiding gossip, reading the Bible, going to small group, or seeking the advice of mentors who love and obey God. I think sometimes we're tempted to equate holiness with perfection, but that's not it at all. Being holy means you pursue a relationship with Jesus Christ through your lifestyle and actions.

> *If we want to be holy—to be set apart—we view our lives as fulfilling a calling, not fulfilling ourselves.*

## 2. Healing

Singleness gives you the space to heal. If you don't take time to get free and get healed of your past wounds, you are building a wall between yourself and your future spouse. This is your time to confront and deal with anything from your past that would hinder your future. The easy way out would be to pretend that your past doesn't bother you and won't hurt you. But no one—and I mean *no one*—is exempt from needing healing and freedom to be all they have the potential to be.

Try praying the prayer, "Lord, I want to heal completely from all that I have been through. Search my heart. Reveal and remove anything in me that is not of you!" This was the first step for me in pursuing a healed heart.

Forgiveness is also an important step in healing. And *you* may be the person you need to forgive. Forgiving someone doesn't offer them absolution, but it does remove our craving for revenge. It's as simple as saying, "You don't owe me anything. I cancel your debt," then moving forward. Now, sometimes it's healthy and wise to say those words out loud to the person who offended or hurt you. But most often, especially when it comes to exes, forgiveness isn't done face-to-face. It's done over time through your own inner workings and prayer.

## 3. Healthy Habits

We are always developing habits, and I believe that a person is what they habitually do. Singleness allows us to develop healthy practices and patterns as individuals. So, what habits are we developing? During our single state, we need to make sure we are developing healthy habits that grow our faith, our confidence, and our leadership and that will lead to growth in our relationships.

Singleness taught me what was really important and what I valued. I want to share some of the healthy habits I learned to develop in my singleness—habits I still have to this day:

- **Prioritize what is important over what is immediate.** If we give in to what we want in the moment, we may find ourselves down a road of resentment and regret later. Our feelings often contradict our values. Singleness is a time to learn how to value what you want most over what you want now. Ask yourself, *What do I really want? What do I really value?* Once I started prioritizing my values and asking myself those hard questions, I became more joyful and content. I became someone I was proud of.

- **Prioritize character over convenience.** Singleness gives you the privilege of becoming the best version of yourself by training your mind not to do whatever is convenient or easy but to do what's right. Oftentimes this means we must go against the crowd (holiness!) and even against our own feelings. That's hard to do, but it will set you apart and set you up for the life you want deep down. There were a lot of moments in my singleness when I wanted to let what felt good or was convenient take over (and there still are!), but because of what I value—becoming who God wants me to be—I'm learning to prioritize doing what's right over what's easy.

- **Prioritize private over public.** I always like to say that who you are when no one is watching is who you will be when everyone is watching. Your private life is your time to build your relationship with Jesus and invest in yourself well. What you put in, how you invest, is what will come out. How much time are you spending investing in yourself? What does your alone time look like?

## IN THE WAITING

I hate waiting.

One time my sisters and I were in line at a concert, waiting to get our tickets scanned. We had been waiting for more than thirty minutes, and the line wasn't moving. We wanted to get to our nachos and Coke, our pictures and T-shirts!

Out of impatience I grabbed my sisters by the hands and

said, "Let's cut in line so we can get in faster." So we acted as if we were going to leave the concert, walking by the long line of people. And then when I saw an opening in the line closer to the front, we jumped right in. The person we cut in front of happened to be intoxicated and not paying much attention. We were in the clear!

I was in the middle of telling my sisters, "I know—I'm a genius. You can thank me later," when a security officer walked up to me and asked if we had cut the line. It's important for you to know that I am the world's worst liar. So with my face getting red and my palms sweating, I stumbled over my words. "Sir, I am not sure what you mean. We have been waiting in line for a very long time with everyone else."

I mean, technically I wasn't lying, right? He seemed content with my answer and was about to walk away when a girl behind us shouted, "They cut in line!"

Like, seriously? Was that completely necessary?

The officer gave me a sour look and took us to the back of the line. Not only did we *not* get our nachos and Coke and T-shirts, but we also missed the entire opening act and even some of the concert.

Needless to say, my sisters did *not* thank me later.

If I hate waiting for these unimportant things, imagine how impatient I am when it comes to the big-moment things. It's bad. But let me tell you what I've learned in those hard-fought waiting seasons: Who I'm becoming in the waiting is more important than what I'm waiting for. In waiting to get in the concert, I became a liar and a cheater. That's not who I am.

> Who I'm becoming in the waiting is more important than what I'm waiting for.

So, how do we wait well? Waiting well means being able to hope for the future that God promises while still being faithful in the season we are currently in. What we learn in the waiting right now prepares us for what will come later. Instead of fixating on leaving the season you are currently in, ask yourself, *What can I learn here that I can use later?* Don't neglect where you currently are because it isn't glamorous or where you want to be.

Like we talked about in chapter 5, singleness isn't a season we endure just so we can get the prize—a husband that completes us. Rather, singleness is a time to become complete in Christ and learn where true love and hope come from: Jesus! It's a time to learn your priorities. And to begin living a life that you can be proud of and that can make a difference.

## IT'S GAME TIME

I grew up playing basketball and I loved game time. Practices, however, weren't my favorite. And don't even get me started on pre-season. But game time, I loved. Game time was filled with adrenaline, loud music, competition, and a crowd in the stands. I was made for it! The only thing I hated about game time was when I would have to come out of the game and sit on the bench, whether because I made a bad play or because I needed to take a break. I felt like I couldn't help my team from the sidelines. Deep down, I knew this wasn't true, because when I was playing, hearing my team cheering for me on the sidelines was all I needed for an ounce of extra effort. But being out of the game, waiting for my name to be called to go back in, was always a dreaded time—even though sometimes I needed that time on the sidelines to regain strength to continue playing and also to build appreciation for when I did get to play.

Singleness can often feel like the sidelines, sitting on the bench, waiting for our name to be called. It can feel like we're just sitting around, wasting time, waiting for our big moment to come. Well, maybe you don't feel this way (and great for you if you don't!), but this is how I used to view it. Singleness was something I dreaded, and I felt like I had nothing to offer as I sat on the sidelines while all my friends played the "game" of marriage.

My mom recently reminded me of a phone call I made to her when I was at a very low point in singleness. "Mom," I said, sobbing, "I think God has forgotten about me."

"Madison," she said, "God hasn't forgotten you. He is preparing you for something so big, you just can't see it right now." She then urged me to start writing my book—*this* book!

I felt like I was on the sidelines while everyone else was in the game. But really, I was in practice—getting ready for what was ahead. If it weren't for that season of singleness, my relationship with Jesus wouldn't be what it is, my confidence wouldn't be where it is, and you wouldn't be reading this book. That season is what birthed in me the dream to start writing.

It took time for my perspective on singleness to change. But the more familiar I grew with the character of God, the more I realized that God is constantly teaching, leading, and growing me. He is a purposeful God. He would never call us into a season of stagnancy, so why was I treating singleness like a never-ending waiting room?

Slowly, I began to realize how active and important a season of singleness should be. It isn't a time of sitting around and waiting. It isn't inactive. Singleness the right way communicates, "I am preparing for the game, and how I perform here will determine how I perform there." If we're insecure and desperate in this season of singleness, why would a season of dating look any different? You practice like you play, right? So how you practice now will determine how you play later.

I will continue emphasizing throughout this book that marriage isn't our ultimate destination. It shouldn't be our biggest goal in life. Therefore, singleness isn't a season of "less than" or a season to pass through quickly as you run toward marriage. Singleness isn't just a vehicle taking you to the perfect destination called marriage. Singleness isn't a problem to be solved by marriage. If you aren't content single, you won't be content married. Why? Because contentment isn't found in a relationship with another imperfect human.

> *Our security doesn't come from a spouse; our security comes from a Savior.*

As a single, you aren't running around as half a person, waiting and hoping for someone to complete you so that you can finally start living. Like we talked about in chapter 5, our security doesn't come from a spouse; our security comes from a Savior.

Singleness *is* a gift. It's given to us at the right time, for a specific purpose. If you're single and you still feel a void, invite God to fill it with the things, people, and habits that are pleasing to him. These kinds of prayers can feel scary because they can feel like we're giving up control. But ultimately, control was never ours to begin with—a fact we should be grateful for.

Why? Because the One who has control has the entire picture laid out in front of him. We receive only one puzzle piece at a time. As a dearly loved child of God, you can rest assured that regardless of what season you're in, you're right where you belong.

> [God] has planned an entire life for you. . . . I pray you won't miss out on the entire story waiting for one chapter.
>
> —LAURA MICHAEL

**BONUS CONTENT**

Using your smartphone,
scan the code for bonus content.

waterbrookmultnomah.com/the-love
-everybody-wants-chapter-10-bonus-content

# 11

## DRIVE BEFORE YOU BUY
### Pursuing Purity Protects Purpose

> How far is too far?
>
> If we don't have sex before marriage, what if it's bad in marriage?
>
> Is it bad to watch pornography?
>
> How do I deal with the shame for everything I've already done?

Anyone would tell you to test-drive a car before you pay a big chunk of cash for it. Get to know how it feels on the road. The bumps, the turns, the brakes. Take it out for a spin. And chances are, you've heard the same idea applied to relationships. "Drive it before you buy it." "See if you are compatible." "Test out your chemistry." Or more frankly, "Sleep with your significant other before you marry him to make sure things will go okay down the road."

I won't lie—I worried about some of those issues because of my commitment to purity before marriage. I even had thoughts like, *Am I going to know what to do in marriage if I don't*

*learn while dating? Would a guy ever want me if I'm not experienced?*
Growing up, I just stayed away from sex because I thought
God would hate me if I didn't. It wasn't until I entered my
twenties that I developed the right view of sex.

Before we go on, I want to say I know this can be a hard
topic for a lot of people. If you haven't lived in purity up to
this point, there is no judgment. This is a safe place. Maybe
you've made decisions you regret out of pressure or temptation. Or maybe you never saw sex as a big deal, and everyone
around you was having sex, so you thought, *Why not?* Maybe
your innocence and purity were taken from you without con-
sent. If you've been raped or abused in any way, I am angered
and sorrowful for you. It is unacceptable and horrible.

Please know that this chapter is meant to express, "Come
as you are, be you, and share your heart," not "Fix yourself,
clean yourself up, and do as I say." We all have a past. We all
have made decisions we aren't very proud of. I am not here to
judge you or tell you what you
should or shouldn't do. To be
honest, I don't care what decisions you've made in the past.

*The past is the past for a reason.*

But I do care about you and the future God has for you. The
past is the past for a reason.

You can't change it. But you can choose where you go from
here.

I am hopeful that this chapter will be encouraging, challenging, and healing, wherever you find yourself.

Maybe you haven't faced those kinds of real temptations
and pressures yet. Maybe for you, steamy romance novels or

pornography led to masturbation, which has been your outlet and escape, your way of numbing yourself or your way of feeling something, even if just for a second. Perhaps you've made the decision to wait for marriage, and you've stayed true to your convictions, but people around you don't understand it and mock you, so you doubt. Maybe you always wanted to pursue purity, but you started dating someone who doesn't value it and doesn't understand it, so little by little you've given more of yourself away. Or maybe you never really saw the value of purity. You never understood why people would wait to have sex. You saw abstaining as odd or pointless.

Wherever you are, whatever has happened up to this point in your life, please know that grace and love meet you right there. And if it's shame and guilt and regret that meet you there, you are at the wrong door, listening to the wrong voice. God loves you, and he cares for you more than you can even imagine. But I will say in truth, he loves you so much that he will meet you where you are but he won't leave you there. He wants to take you higher. He wants to make you better. He will call you deeper because he wants you to experience the abundant life he has to offer.

So, as you read through this chapter, I hope you know that even if you haven't made many decisions that you are proud of and you feel like, "What's the point? I already lost my virginity. It doesn't matter now," that's a lie. It does matter. Your heart matters. Your spirit matters. Your body matters. Your future matters. You can't change the past, but you can change what your future looks like. You can decide today to honor God, yourself, and your future spouse.

## MY FIRST CAR

When I got my first car, it was Christmas Day, and my parents sent me on a scavenger hunt. One clue leading to the next—I was so anxious to see what I got! My mom videoed my every movement. My sisters followed me around eagerly. My dad was just proud to be there. We were all in our matching pajamas, which was our Christmas tradition. I had no idea what to expect, but I knew it had to be something big because the video camera was out!

I finally got the last clue, and it led me to the driveway. I couldn't believe it. An all-white car with a big, shiny red bow. I thought, *This is for me?* My sister Mallory started crying. She was so happy for me. I couldn't believe my parents pulled off such a big surprise without me finding out! And, of course, I couldn't believe they got me a car! I was so thrilled and shocked. I immediately began thinking about the playlists I was going to make for late-night drives with my friends. I hugged my parents tightly. I wanted them to feel my appreciation. I opened the driver's door, sat down inside, and took a deep breath. It had that new-car smell!

I sat in the car for hours, just taking it in. Then I adjusted my rearview mirror, scooted up my seat, and pulled out of the driveway. I remember thinking, *This car is perfect. It's everything I love in a car and exactly what I would have picked out. It drives like a dream!*

But I want to make a point here. I didn't have to test-drive the car first, because my dad did. My dad went to the dealership, looked at all the options, drove the car around, and decided, *Yup, this one is made for Madi!* My dad knew exactly what I wanted and, more importantly, what I needed. And how much more does your heavenly Father know exactly what you need? He knows every desire of your heart—he put the desires there! And let me tell you, when you trust your Father to give you exactly what you need, it's always better than what you could have ever picked out for yourself.

One day on social media I made a post about how I was saving myself for marriage, and to my surprise, when I checked the post, I read more than a thousand comments telling me that I was stupid and I should always "test-drive a car before I buy it." I started to think about that analogy. Our society truly believes this principle when it comes to sex and purity—comparing a partner to something as disposable as a vehicle. It identifies the other person as worthy of love only if they perform well enough. It also insinuates that sex is not just a deciding factor but *the* make-or-break factor. Yet there are many, many other aspects of marriage that should be prioritized over sex. Marriage lasts your whole life; sex does not.

> *Marriage lasts your whole life; sex does not.*

Also, we buy a car to get us from one location to the next; it's something we use when we need it. Not to mention, it's something we trade out five to ten years later when we get tired of it or the engine stops working. No human being is meant to be compared to a vehicle. If you connect with someone emotionally, intellectually, and spiritually, connecting with them physically will be natural and beautiful. And if not at first, you have trust, friendship, good communication, and understanding to improve all aspects of your relationship.

Do you remember your first kiss? (If you've had one already! ☺) I remember mine like it was yesterday. I could tell you exactly what I was wearing, where I was standing, and why I was there. I was fifteen years old. He was my first boyfriend. We had been dating for a few months. All of my friends were getting their first kiss, and, well, I'm competitive. So, I might have hinted to him that I was ready for a kiss (quite a few times, knowing me). One night, outside my friend's house at exactly 9:30 P.M., he grabbed my hand and leaned in for a kiss. I was in jeans and an Abercrombie tee. Iconic. My hair was straightened and pulled back by a bobby pin. I had on blue eyeshadow and light pink lipstick. (Why was this allowed? How was that cute?) Anyway, I got my kiss. I felt on top of the world!

I immediately told all my friends. I was so proud and excited. He and I continued dating, and kissing became less about goosebumps and fireworks and more about leading into something else. This thing that I thought was so magical and beautiful became normal and led my boyfriend to push other boundaries that I felt uncomfortable with.

After he and I broke up a few months later, I went on to date other guys throughout high school. With each relationship, boundaries would get pushed, and I would feel something tugging my heart that I couldn't deny. I knew I was supposed to stay away from sex and save it for my husband, but what about the other stuff? This was something I wrestled with. When boundaries were pushed, I would justify it in my head or even be told by the guy, "It's not that big of a deal, Madi. It's such a small thing." But every time I gave in, I would feel shame and insecurity, like I was being robbed of my identity, strength, and purpose.

To be honest, for the longest time, my idea of purity and "saving myself" was fear based because I didn't want to disappoint anyone. I didn't want to let my parents down or even myself down as I strove to have the perfect reputation. My view of purity was even prideful; I thought God would bless me more if I somehow followed all his "rules." So, it's not surprising to me when I hear that people find waiting until marriage too hard. Not many people are willing to lay down their wants and needs to follow rules. And I don't blame them. I'm not either. But many would be willing to lay down wants and needs for real love. Yet most of us haven't been presented with this idea of purity being an act of love and protection.

When Grant and I started dating, we realized quickly how passionate we were for each other and how slippery that slope was. So, we decided to make a purity contract. Think what you want, but we did what we had to do! The contract was a commitment from us both to complete purity, honoring God and each other, individually and together. We signed it and sent it to our mentors and accountability partners. But let me just tell you, we were not perfect and there were moments when that contract was nearly broken because of "small" moments of compromise.

Those moments led to intense confusion, division, and anxiety. We even took a break one time as a result. One moment of pleasure isn't worth weeks, months, or even a lifetime of regret and resentment. Anytime Grant and I crossed a line, I didn't feel closeness. I felt shame and insecurity. It brought doubt into the relationship. And for weeks we would feel foggy, which would lead to more sin and anger. We would be short-tempered and quick to blame and attack the other. Until we got to the place where we finally just said, "It's not worth it."

Once we came to that conclusion, our relationship grew stronger than ever. Our communication was better. We gained clarity on the relationship. We grew in trust, respect, and love for each other. We became best friends on the deepest level. Today, with everything in our hearts, we want to encourage everyone that purity is so worth it. It may be the hardest commitment to keep, but it will change your life and relationship. It changed ours. When we fully pursued purity, Grant became more confident and led well spiritually. I became more free and joyful, trusting in his leadership.

Here's the thing—sex and all sexual acts were created to be experienced in the confines of marriage and to bring unity to the marriage. But when we experience them outside the covenant of marriage, they bring the opposite—all the destructive consequences Grant and I experienced and, sometimes, irrecoverable devastation. This is true for any sexual acts, not just sex. Anything done that arouses you. Whatever that means for you. Making out. Lying together on a couch. Talking about certain things.

If you are asking yourself, *Is this too far?* it's too far. Don't try to get as close to the line of impurity as you can. Try to get as close to purity as you can. Crossing the line of impurity or dancing beside it hinders your intimacy with God and your future intimacy with your husband. Chasing purity and holiness with all you've got helps grow your intimacy with God and your future intimacy with your husband.

## PURITY IS ABOUT MORE THAN SEX

Purity is so much more than waiting until marriage to have sex and sexual pleasure. Purity is a mindset; it's a heart posture; it's a lifestyle. It's not a box we can check, striving our best to achieve and perform, playing under the rules of pass/fail. Purity has to be viewed as something bigger and deeper than that, or else it won't be valued or protected.

When I was thirteen, I was introduced to pornography by a couple of my friends in middle school. I remember what it made me feel, what it did to my body, and the warped picture of sex and relationships it instilled in me. For many months after that, I battled with the temptation of pornography.

I didn't think pornography was something girls were supposed to struggle with, and I assumed lust was only a man's struggle. I wrestled with self-hatred and shame because of this, thinking I was the only girl in the world fighting the temptation to watch pornography. And for years, I carried this shame, feeling dirty, as if I'd permanently damaged my purity.

One day a friend shared with me how much she regretted giving herself to a random guy she met in college. After that, she began exploring her sexuality through pornography. It became such an intense addiction that she couldn't go a day without it, and she craved it. She didn't tell anyone, and this secret addiction consumed her life and thoughts and hindered her joy, confidence, and relationships. She couldn't find contentment in anything else because the high that virtual sex brought her in the moment dulled everything in real life. One day she hit rock bottom when she realized she had completely lost herself and isolated herself because of her addiction and the shame that came with it. She didn't know what else to do, so she went to church. While there, she met and connected with other people in her stage of life. She started meeting a particular girl for coffee. Over time, my friend confessed her secret addiction. She hadn't told anyone before. But when she shared it, she felt the shackles fall off. Of course, her addiction didn't go away at that moment, but through accountability and with the help of God's Spirit, she overcame it and now shares her story with so many people.

When my friend shared this story with me, I immediately felt comforted. I wasn't alone. I shared with her my struggles and my past with pornography, and I began to weep. I had never told anyone. And in that moment, saying it out loud to someone who understood and wasn't judging me, I felt hope for the first time. After confessing it, I, too, felt the soul ties break. I felt the label of lust and shame disappear. I felt hopeful again. I felt myself again.

If this is your struggle, too, I hope you know that you are not alone, and I want you to understand that you don't have to let this label or dependence rob you anymore. Find someone trustworthy—someone who loves God and loves you—and confess. Healing and freedom and accountability are found in confession. You were made to love and to be loved.

You were made to live and to live to the fullest. You weren't made to find satisfaction from a computer or phone screen.

The good news is that God's grace covers all your sins and shortcomings. He can redeem the most broken and messy parts of your heart and life. I don't care what you have done or what has been done to you—God can redeem it, restore it, and use it to help and free others. And if you are in a relationship and you have failed and failed again, don't give up hope and throw in the towel. God isn't mad at you or disappointed. In fact, Romans 5:8 says, "God demonstrates his own love for us in this: While we were still sinners, Christ died for us."

God loves you so much, right now, just as you are. He loves you so much that he wants purity for you from this point forward because he wants you free, healed, whole, joyful, peaceful, and innocent again! Picture yourself as a little kid, running around with bliss, joy, and innocence. That is what pursuing purity brings.

Purity is protection. Purity guards our hearts and our bodies. Purity has made it easier for me to make decisions and use discernment. Purity is a *gift* we're given, not a list of requirements to get to heaven. I think for so long our culture has painted purity as a list of what you can't have. That's not been my experience at all. Purity has given me far more than it's taken away.

Too often when the topic of purity is brought up, it's within

> You were made to love and to be loved. You were made to live and to live to the fullest. You weren't made to find satisfaction from a computer or phone screen.

the context of rules or reprimands. We walk away feeling hopeless, like the rules are impossible to follow and we've already failed. I'm here to tell you, even if no one else has, God didn't encourage you in the way of purity to set you up for failure and rob you of fun or pleasure. Rather, as the creator of pleasure itself, he challenges you and me to pursue purity to preserve our future—to preserve our future intimacy, our hearts' health, our discernment. God wants to give us something, not withhold it. The idea of purity has become a joke to many, yet those same individuals wonder why their lives are so full of anxiety, anger, hopelessness, and relational disappointment. I can assure you, following God's way is always in your best interest, for your own protection and future pleasure!

Fighting for purity is not popular, and it's not easy. None of the movies that make it onto the big screen are presenting this message. I would guess that most of your friends aren't either. Social media definitely isn't. Don't let the pressure to compromise, cave, and conform keep you from living a life of conviction and clarity. I believe that for you and me to find the love we want, a commitment to purity is essential.

> Don't let the pressure to compromise, cave, and conform keep you from living a life of conviction and clarity.

## THE GOOD DIFFERENT

I remember going to a party first semester of my freshman year of college. I saw a cute guy and we started flirting. He asked me to come over and watch a movie after the party, so I let my friends know and told them I would be fine. I guess I was ignorant, but I truly thought he wanted to watch a movie with me.

When we got back to his apartment, he went straight to his bedroom and took all his clothes off. I was so taken aback, I yelled out, "What are you doing?"

He responded, "What did you expect?"

I threw his pants and shirt at him and said, "Put your clothes back on."

He finally gave in and got dressed, but he continued trying to force himself on me. I continued pushing him off until he finally gave up. He proceeded to lie down and fall asleep. I realized it was three o'clock in the morning and I was in this random guy's apartment with no way home. None of my friends would answer their phones. I was stuck. I waited up all night, praying to the Lord to send someone to help me. Especially before the guy woke up. Finally, around six in the morning, one of my friends responded and came to pick me up.

I got back to my dorm room, and I hit my knees. I began crying and praying. That situation was traumatizing and uncomfortable. I had never had a guy make a sexual advance toward me before, and I was new to living on my own. As I was praying, I had a moment of realization and awakening: College and life would be full of those moments of pressure and temptation, and I wanted to know how I was going to respond before those situations came. I decided during that prayer time to make a commitment to God and save myself for marriage. Not because I had to or because I was told to.

And not out of fear or pride or guilt. I wanted to from a place of love and sacrifice. That random guy scolded me for not sleeping with him, saying, "Well, you're different from the other girls." I thought, *Good.* I wanted to be different. A *good* different. I wanted to give God all of me. And then one day, if the time came, I would give my husband all of me.

So many of my friends were confused by my decision to save myself. They would laugh and make comments about how much I was missing out. I eventually sat them down and reminded them that I loved them and wasn't judging them for their decisions, but I asked them respectfully to not judge me for mine. I did, however, challenge them, "Whenever you get tired of crying yourself to sleep after hooking up with one guy after another, asking yourself, *Is there more?* and *Will I ever find a love that actually lasts?* just know that I am here and would love to talk about why I am choosing to save myself."

About a week later, one of those friends came up to me and said, "Madi, I really respect what you're doing." She proceeded to tell me her whole story and how empty and broken she felt. She wanted to pursue purity, but she felt like she was already too far gone. She also feared she wouldn't attract guys anymore. She said, "Most guys pursue me for my body and what I can do. What if they don't like me anymore if I stop?"

I got to encourage her and pray over her and remind her that purity was one of the best decisions she could ever make. I told her, "You are so much more than your looks. The right guy, the right love, will see you and want you for who you truly are. And choosing to save yourself shouldn't be from a place of 'have to' or feeling like you are giving up a life of fun and passion and now you have to live this boring life until you get married. It's the opposite. It's full. It's purposeful. It's joyful. It's free."

She ended up making the decision to save herself for her husband. Years later, when she got married, she came up to me after her rehearsal dinner with tears in her eyes and said, "Thank you, Madi. I have never been happier. I have never been more at peace. Purity was so worth it."

It wasn't always easy for my friend. It wasn't always easy for me. Pressures from other people and even from within are hard to withstand. And the truth is, people won't understand a life of purity. Social media won't understand a life of purity. You will be seen as different, uncommon, and maybe even weird. But it's a good different. It's a set-apart different. However, it's got to be more than mere hype, talk, or intention. There must be action steps. All day long we can talk about the benefits and importance of pursuing purity, but if there is no direction or discipline, it's pointless. It's simply motivation without action. I don't want to just give you something that motivates. I want to give you something that encourages, challenges, or transforms you.

So, let's talk about it. How do you remain pure? What are your boundaries? Here are some ideas that have helped me:

- **Pray for forgiveness and confess for healing.** The Bible tells us to pray to be forgiven and then confess to be healed. James 5:16 says, "Confess your sins to each other and pray for each other so that you may be healed." For us to live lives of freedom and purity, we need to break free from the bondage of sin and addiction. Repent, ask God to forgive you, and commit to pursuing purity and living a life of honor and holiness. Confess to a godly friend, mentor, or pastor, and have them pray over you so that you may be healed from the past.

- **Know your why.** Your why is your reason for having boundaries in the first place—the principles you can return to again and again to reinforce your resolve. I've learned through trial and error, heartache, and doing things my own way that God's will is best. My why is because I want God's best for me *and* his best for the man I love. You may be able to withstand temptation for a season, but knowing why it's worth it to maintain your boundaries will be critical in the long haul. Remind yourself of your why regularly, not just in the heat of the moment. And remind yourself of why God says pursuing purity is important. Daily ask, *Is my lifestyle aligning with God's Word? Am I honoring God with my choices, body, and relationships?* Think about 1 Thessalonians 4:3: "This is the will of God, your sanctification: that you abstain from sexual immorality" (esv).

- **Pre-decide your boundaries and tell someone.** Decide before you find yourself in the heat of the moment. Don't leave it up to fate or feelings, because most of the time they will let you down. After you've decided your boundaries, tell someone. Bring accountability or mentorship into that decision. Find a friend who is spiritually on the same level or a step ahead of you to hold you accountable. My best friend and roommate had access to my purity contract with Grant and would ask me after every date if we stayed true to it and to our convictions. It held me accountable because she not only knew my boundaries but would also ask me the hard questions when I came home. Someone needs to know what your boundaries are. Live in the light!

- **Surround yourself with godly friends.** Surround yourself with people who love you and love God even more. They will be a solid source of wisdom and counsel when you need it most. In college I had a group of six girls that I did life with, and we all challenged one another to pursue purity and to pursue Jesus in our day-to-day lives. We had weekly gatherings in our living rooms where we would confess to, pray for, and encourage one another. Having accountability *and* constant encouragement goes far. Remember, you naturally become more like the people you spend the most time with. We're still friends to this day, and I've made it a priority to have friends around me that will call me higher, challenge me to walk in the will of God, and encourage me in my faith and convictions. We're told in Proverbs 13:20 that if our friends are wise, we will become wise too. If you're the only person in your friend group pursuing purity, you may find yourself losing motivation or conviction because you're the odd one out.

- **Resist the itch.** Were you told when you were younger the danger of scratching your bug bite? If you keep scratching the itch, it could lead to scarring or infection. The only way that bite goes away is if you resist the itch. Resisting the itch is hard because those first few scratches feel good and don't seem to cause much harm. Which is *not* unlike our sinful cravings! They start small and don't seem to be that big of a deal, until we realize we've gone too far and it's cost us more than we expected. The itch *can* go away if you resist it. This resistance takes persistence and discipline. In order to stop having sex with your boyfriend or to stop watching porn or to stop having sexual thoughts, you have to resist the itch and do so with intensity and intentionality. For me, I had to remove apps from my phone, give up my computer, and watch only PG movies to resist the itch to watch something I shouldn't. When I was dating Grant, I had to set a curfew, text a friend for accountability, recognize our temptation triggers (being together late at night or lying down on a couch together), and put up boundaries.

- **Feed the spirit.** What you feed and nurture grows. Have you ever planted a flower or tended a garden before? It takes intentionality. It takes nurturing. It's the same thing for your spirit. It isn't going to grow by itself. For Jesus to increase and your sinful nature to decrease, you must feed that spirit inside you. Spend more time in God's Word, in godly community, and in prayer and worship than you do on social media or alone in your bedroom.

- **Pray for strength.** Honestly, we all need to pray for supernatural vision, discipline, and strength to remain pure. What feels impossible *is* possible with God.

This may all feel overwhelming, but I have found it is worth it to choose discipline over regret and to pursue purity to protect my purpose and relationships. And I'm not arguing that purity is easy. Nothing worthwhile in life will ever be easy. Everything worthwhile will come with a fight. But what comes out of it will bless you and your future relationships in ways you could never imagine.

> Blessed are the pure in heart,
> for they will see God.
> —Matthew 5:8

**BONUS CONTENT**

Using your smartphone,
scan the code for bonus content.

waterbrookmultnomah.com/the-love
-everybody-wants-chapter-11-bonus-content

# 12

## CHECKING ALL THE BOXES
### Dating with Purpose

*How do I know what to look for?*
*How can I date well?*
*What is the point of dating?*

I can't tell you how many questions I've heard along these lines. Or how many books I've read and how many podcasts and sermons I've listened to all on the topic of dating. Dating is confusing. Dating is hard. I haven't always dated well. But is it any wonder we all struggle? Most advice for relationships today is found in social media, TV shows, movies, and music—which rarely show us what it looks like to date purposefully or have healthy and holy relationships.

One of the biggest questions I asked was, "How do I know what to look for?" I wrestled with this constantly. "Will I just know?" "Should I make a list and see if he checks the boxes?" Ironically, about two years ago, in the middle of debating this question, I got asked to come and speak at a church on this exact topic. As I prepared my talk, I asked myself, *Yeah, what do you look for?* I had always said I knew what I wanted in a spouse but had never taken the time to actually write it down. I sat on it for a while, and three things kept coming up. They are what I now call my three C's—the three things I needed to see before I even considered dating someone.

## THE THREE C'S

Sounds a little intense, but I knew what I deserved and what I had prayed for and waited for. So, for me to be called some-one's girlfriend, these three things had to be checked off.

### 1. Convictions

As I mentioned in chapter 8, a conviction is "a firmly held belief or opinion." When we're interested in a guy, it's important that we evaluate his convictions. Not his mom's and dad's convictions or how he was raised or if he wears a cross necklace or if he has been to church before or if he owns a Bible. I mean, who is he in Christ? What is his core belief about who Jesus is, on good days and bad days? Does he set an example in faith? Does his life display that his relationship with Jesus is his top priority? Does he live on a mission to love Jesus and love people? Is he led by his convictions over his feelings and flesh?

Anyone can think something and say something all day long, but do his actions follow his beliefs? In other words, does he live out his convictions?

I know those are a lot of questions to think through, but it's important that before you even consider dating someone, you see that person as someone with strong convictions that align with yours. If dating is for evaluating the possibility of marriage, that means that dating is to be taken seriously. I would encourage you to not give someone your heart, your time, or your attention until you know their convictions.

## 2. Character

*Character* has many definitions, but this is one I heard a lot growing up: "Character is who you are when no one's looking." Character says, "I do the thing I know is right, not what I feel like doing." Character is being bigger on the inside than the outside. It's usually born in private, built through opposition, and strengthened through suffering.

Ask yourself, *Does this guy have godly character? Is he someone who will help shape my character in a healthy way? When opportunities to bend the truth or cut a corner arise, what does he do? What kind of example does he set in his speech? Do his words bring life and encouragement? Is he a man of his word?*

Character is also defined by having good traits: selflessness, generosity, honesty, faithfulness, kindness, empathy, courage, responsibility, wisdom, humility, teachability. Having good character isn't just about winning the approval of people; it's also about pleasing and honoring God. And character doesn't appear overnight. It has to be grown. It has to be practiced. Daily.

## 3. Chemistry

Let me just start off saying there is a difference between lustful attraction and godly attraction. Lustful chemistry is led by sinful cravings. Lust is what the self desires. Lustful chemistry says, "We have to test the waters to see if this will work." So, hear me: I am not telling you to find someone who gets your blood pumping and whose shirt you want to rip off.

However, I do think when you find someone who has strong character and convictions, he naturally becomes attractive to you. Attraction is often based on what we see first. We see someone our eyes like, and usually our feelings follow. But character and convictions are what keep us there. Of course, you want to enjoy looking at the face of the person you hope to be with for the rest of your life. I personally don't agree with "Just go find anyone who loves God, and you can make it work." I mean, that might be true. But I'd rather find an attractive man spiritually, physically, and emotionally.

Those were the three things I preached on during that service, and I had so many people come up to me saying how helpful it was for them. Several began sharing about their relationships and asking for advice and prayer. (Many tag me still to this day, talking about the three C's!)

I walked away from that experience, and the word *foundation* kept coming to mind. It made me start thinking about my living situation at the time—a newly renovated older house in Dallas. About a month in, my roommate and I started having problem after problem with the house. Our floors kept rising, creating uneven and cracked surfaces. There were parts of our house you could literally skateboard down; we had our own built-in ramps! The landlord had people fix the floors, but soon the same issues would return.

This continued for more than a year. We couldn't understand what was going on. We kept getting so frustrated . . . until we realized it wasn't a floor issue. It was a foundation issue. Our foundation was bad, causing a lot of other problems and headaches in our home. No matter how much we tried to fix the issues, they just kept occurring because of the bad foundation.

If you think about your life and relationships, it always comes back to your foundation. You can't build a relationship on a shaky, uneven foundation. Even if *you* have a solid foundation, if the person you're dating or hoping to date doesn't have a solid foundation in Jesus, the relationship isn't going to last. Or maybe it will, but all you will get is problems and headaches.

## THREE QUESTIONS TO CONSIDER

When I found a guy I was interested in and I could see all three C's, I then liked to ask myself three questions as I continued dating and evaluating him:

1. **Does he make me more like Jesus?** This has to do with *identity:* I want to reflect the heart of Jesus. We are going to naturally become like those we surround ourselves with. So, who am I becoming when I'm with this guy? Do I like who I'm becoming? Am I becoming more like Christ?

2. **Does he push me closer to Jesus?** This has to do with *faith:* I want to be as close to Jesus as possible. I want my relationship with God to be the strongest and most impor-

tant relationship in my life. What do I believe about Jesus when I'm with this guy? After spending time with him, do I feel closer to Jesus or further from him? Does this guy cause me to compromise, or does he challenge me to uphold my convictions and standards?

3. **Does he help me make a difference for Jesus?** This has to do with *purpose:* I want to make a difference with and for Jesus. Do I do more for the kingdom of God when I'm with this guy? Can we do more together than we could do separately? Does he help me love and serve other people well?

If the relationship is God-honoring, it will make you want to be better every single day. It will challenge you and inspire you to be the best version of yourself.

## LOOK FOR A LEADER

> If the relationship is God-honoring, it will make you want to be better every single day. It will challenge you and inspire you to be the best version of yourself.

If you can see all three C's and you can answer "Yes!" to all the questions above, next you need to evaluate the two of you together. Ask yourself, *Even if he has what it takes to be my man, does he want to be my man?*

He can have all the right qualities all day long, but if he isn't willing to work for you, he's not the one for you. One of my friends constantly felt frustrated

by her boyfriend's lack of pur-
suit. She would express to him
the ways he was making her feel
unsafe and unloved and the
things she would like him to do
for her to feel safer and more
pursued. He went on to tell her that if he didn't feel like it and
it didn't come naturally to him, he couldn't do it.

Ask yourself, Even if he has what it takes to be my man, does he want to be my man?

It left me frustrated for her because that is an immature
and selfish view of love. To love is to lay your life down for the
other person, to sacrifice and serve even when you don't feel
like it. She continued in the relationship because he was a
good guy who loved God. Eventually I told her, "He may have
what it takes to be your man, but that doesn't mean that he
wants to do what it takes to be your man." She kept trying to
make it work, and they were together for more than a year.
When the relationship came to an end, it hurt her. But I encouraged her that temporary heartbreak is much better than
a lifetime of regret and resentment. You should never have to
beg someone to want you and love you.

So ask yourself . . .

1. Is he capable of leading you?
2. Does he want to lead you?

Both are important. You can't just have one. One shows his
willingness to fight for you and love you. The other shows his
ability to respect you and lead you. He may want you, but he

may not deserve you. You have to ask, Is he the man for the job? How well does he lead himself? How well does he lead those around him? Is he easily led by his feelings? By his cravings? By the crowd? Or is he a leader that chooses to be led by his convictions? (The answers to these questions will determine if he can lead you.)

> *He may want you, but he may not deserve you.*

## DATING WELL

Let's face it: Dating is tricky. Even if you're trying to date the right way, it's hard to find someone else who's trying to do it the right way too. Finding two people on the same page is hard.

I really had to grow in some areas before I was ready to date the right way. Let me share a story about one area I had to change.

In my senior year of high school, we took votes for senior superlatives. I was excited to see which I would get. Maybe best dressed? Best looking? Most athletic? Most popular? I was hoping for those. The results came back, and I couldn't believe the two I got: biggest flirt and best Christian example. What a combination! Biggest flirt? Come on! It totally wasn't what I was going for. I asked all my friends, "Am I really that flirty?"

They all rolled their eyes. "Yes, Madi!" I had no idea. No wonder the guys I dated in high school would get so irritated with me and jealous.

As I got older and began to date with the intention to marry, I had to take my propensity to flirt seriously. I didn't want to be a flirty girl. I wanted to be a loyal girl. I didn't want to be easily available to anyone. I wanted to save myself for one person. Even in the way I talked and dressed.

When Grant and I started dating, we had a lot to overcome. (Funny, I later found out he also got voted biggest flirt in high school. So, I guess you could say we were on the same page!) Through a lot of failing, learning, and growing together, we finally found a rhythm and learned how to honor the other person and date well. Here is our advice for how to "check all the boxes" in dating on purpose.

## 1. Date Prayerfully

This may sound basic or even silly to you, but this is one of the best things you can do for your relationship. To clarify, I don't mean hold hands and pray together as if you're husband and wife. I mean you should both be individually praying and also have accountability partners and mentors around you praying. I grew up believing that prayer is powerful and can quite literally change things. I learned that from my mom. She prayed over my relationships. If she didn't think I was dating a man after God's heart, she would intensify her prayer even more. I finally looked at her and said, "I am thankful you are praying the wrong ones out, but do you mind praying the right one in?"

Right before I met Grant, my mom had a feeling I was going to meet my husband soon. When I met Grant, she assured me, "This is the man I have prayed for." But I wasn't just living off my mom's prayers. I was on my knees praying. Praying for my heart. Praying for God to develop me and cleanse me of any impurity or ill intention. Long before Grant even came into the picture, I had been praying for God to make me into a woman of godly character and to prepare my heart to be a wife.

Within my relationship with Grant, we had moments when we would struggle or fight, and I didn't know if we were going to get married or break up. In those times, I would just start praying. And every single time, God would give me the grace and peace I needed to keep going and keep loving. If it weren't for prayer, I don't know that we would be here! Prayer is powerful and effective. Prayer can change things.

## 2. Date Purposefully

Everything done well is done intentionally. Relationships don't just turn out great because everything in life is easy and perfect. Relationships are hard work. That is why this chapter's subtitle isn't "Date Perfectly." The goal is to date with purpose. Date on mission. Date in a way that makes you both better and the people around you better. Date in a way that honors your values and beliefs. Date with vision and clarity. Make it known where you want to go.

## 3. Date in Purity

We've already hit on this in chapter 11, but purity is so important for a relationship to be all that God created it to be. When we miss this step or choose to ignore it, we rob ourselves of the abundance of joy, freedom, and love that we could have. And that doesn't mean that if purity hasn't been a part of your relationship, you're just going to have a less abundant life. God's favor isn't rewards based. He doesn't give you greater blessing because of your merit and efforts. Purity isn't to take something from you. However, purity is for your own protection.

Confidence in God takes the desperation out of dating. We tend to overcomplicate things. I hope this chapter helped simplify things for you so that if and when you find yourself in a season of dating, you can know how to date with purpose. I want to also remind you that dating isn't something to glorify or idolize, nor is marriage. You don't need anyone else to fulfill you. Only God can. The desire to be loved and get married isn't a bad desire, yet it shouldn't become the ultimate goal in your heart.

*Confidence in God takes the desperation out of dating.*

> Dating with an eye toward marriage changes not just when you date and who you date but also how you date.
>
> —JONATHAN POKLUDA, *Outdated*

## BONUS CONTENT

Using your smartphone,
scan the code for bonus content.

waterbrookmultnomah.com/the-love
-everybody-wants-chapter-12-bonus-content

# 13

## SEASON, REASON, OR LIFETIME?
### Defining the Relationship

> Why am I not getting what I want quickly?
> Why don't my relationships last?
> Am I a failure if my relationship fails?

We are impatient people. Modern conveniences haven't helped us cultivate a spirit of patience. "I want what I want as soon as I want it"—this is what my heart seems to say constantly. But that kind of driving desire, when left unfulfilled, can lead to increasing frustration and, in some cases, even panic. When this kind of panic sets in, we will take whatever is within arm's reach, even if it isn't God's best for us.

There is a season for everything under heaven (Ecclesiastes 3:1). When we release our grip of our own timelines, we can rest in his sovereignty and stop feeling so panicky about our relationship status. Confidence in God takes the desperation out of searching.

It's just like in Justin Bieber's song "Lifetime," where he

> Confidence in God takes the desperation out of searching.

said, "Some people come in your life for a reason. Others, they come in your life for a season." Then he went on to sing about his wife: "But, baby, you are a lifetime."[1] We all desire lifetime relationships. We aren't wired to be happy about having people come into our lives and then exit quickly. However, I've learned throughout my life so far that some people serve a purpose for a season, some leave for a reason, and others are meant to be with you for a lifetime.

When it comes to romantic relationships, obviously our goal and hope most often is to find someone who fits in that lifetime category. Not long ago, I was genuinely ready to find my person to settle down with and do life with forever. Up until that point, I had moments when I had to let go of a person I thought might have been the one. I had moments of being rejected, walked out on, and cheated on. I had moments of finding a great guy who checked all the boxes but lacking peace and joy about the relationship. And then I had a moment when it felt like God blessed the broken road that led me into the loving arms of Grant Michael Troutt, my lifetime.

The journey to this point felt long, confusing, frustrating, lonely, and hopeless—but it was ultimately worth it. I want to encourage you, wherever you find yourself, and give you reassurance about why some relationships must end.

But first, fun fact about me: I've caught fifteen wedding bouquets. I even caught one on national television. There is a picture of me catching one of the bouquets, and I'm ten feet in the air, over everyone else's head. My eyes were so locked in and intense. And the people around me were shrinking back in fear because of my intensity and aggression. I saved those bridal bouquets for a long time, but then there were just dead flowers all over my house, and it was too much.

How could I have caught so many? Well, for starters, I'm extremely competitive. And second, I desperately wanted to find my lifetime person. The whole idea of catching the bouquet is that you're getting married next. I thought, *The more I catch, the better chance I have!* It didn't quite work like that. I started catching these bouquets in 2016, but I didn't get married until 2022. I think I was a bridesmaid in ten weddings during those six years. And likely attended another twenty on top of that.

During those six years, I experienced heartbreak, rejection, closed doors, and a lot of waiting. I tried with everything I had to get married on my timeline. Even by catching fifteen bouquets. But relationships don't always end the way we want them to. And I don't mean to sound discouraging, but there is way more of a chance that relationships won't work out than that they will. It might take many tries. Or maybe if you're lucky, you will find your lifetime guy the first try. Dating doesn't always look the way we want it to or turn out the way we expected, but there is always a purpose in it and a lesson to be learned.

Sometimes people aren't meant to be in our lives forever, but everyone in our lives is there for a purpose and can teach us something. What if a person was put into your life to prepare you? To guide you? To protect you? Even though it might not have worked out romantically and you may not always understand in the moment, you will be stronger and wiser because of it. It makes me think of something a mentor once told me: "The peace God gives far exceeds the understanding you think you have to have."

## THERE'S A SEASON FOR EVERYTHING

Ecclesiastes 3:1 tells us there's a season for everything. And it's true. God created the world with seasons, which means they are inevitable. We weren't meant to just experience one season for our whole lives. Just as earth has seasons, our lives have seasons like mourning, dancing, breaking, building, refining, and redeeming. Without the hard seasons, would the good seasons be as good? Without the mourning, would the rejoicing be as great? Without the losses and failures, would the victory be as rewarding? Without the darkness of night, would the bright light of day be as sweet? Without the cold and stormy winter, would the spring and summer bring as much joy? We all go through seasons in life, just like we do in relationships. People may come into your life for a season, but maybe they weren't meant to stay.

Maybe you met a friend your first semester of college who helped you come out of your shell. You don't talk anymore because you grew apart, but for a time, that friendship was necessary to your becoming. I've had many seasonal friendships. And it's always hard growing apart from someone. But when you can look back and see the purpose they served in your life—and you in theirs—it's helpful.

Even though I had my years of boy obsession, I've had only three relationships that played big roles in my becoming. The first one was for a reason. The second one was for a season. This guy came into my life for a season and brought healing and hope to my life again. God also used him to reveal a lot of selfishness and pride in my heart that I needed to confront and deal with. But no matter how hard I tried to force it and make it last, he wasn't meant to be my lifetime.

There's a confidence that comes with knowing that there's a season for everything and that each season comes on time. That means you don't have to rush it or force it. So, if you're single right now and you're frustrated with your season of singleness, trust that God's timing is better than yours. Anything you try to create and manipulate with your own hands will only leave you frustrated. I had to get to a place in my life where I was willing to let go, because for so long I wanted my own perfect will on my own timeline. But it left me frustrated, discontent, and unhappy. When I finally got to a place of surrender and trust, I found peace and contentment. I knew deep down that I wanted an "only God" kind of relationship. However, when it started to look different than I thought and the season of singleness lasted longer than I expected, it was easy for me to try to grip what I could, yet it never satisfied, and it didn't last. I knew that if I didn't surrender and trust the God who created me and created the seasons, I wouldn't find my lifetime—rather, I would settle for a season or reason relationship. God's way is so much better. But it requires letting go and trusting him.

## EVERYTHING HAPPENS FOR A REASON

Everyone comes into your life for a reason—good or bad. This can be a substitute teacher who taught you for a day but encouraged you in your writing; you never saw them again, but their words of encouragement led you to your purpose. This can be a coach who trained you all throughout high school and helped you develop a good work ethic. This can be someone who befriended you when you were new and lonely and didn't have anyone else. This can be a significant person, like someone you dated for years but eventually broke up with.

I dated one guy for four years, and I look back at that relationship and call it my "reason relationship." During that time, I learned so much about love and life. We started dating freshman year of college. It was the first real relationship I had ever been in, and I learned so much about how love is a choice and not just an emotion. I look back now, and I believe God used him in my life to protect me from what my wild-at-heart nature may have fallen into if it weren't for him.

Not only was there a reason God brought him into my life, but there was also a reason he took him out of it. God had other plans, better plans, for the both of us. We weren't God's best for each other. When it ended, it was painful. I cried myself to sleep for months. But I kept clinging to Romans 8:28, which talks about how God works everything together for good. I felt deep within that what was meant for me would be mine, without me forcing or controlling anything.

I believe that there's a reason for everything you walk through. The good and bad can both serve a purpose. Even if you've walked through traumatic experiences, God can redeem them and use them for good. Pain can serve a purpose, too, if you bring it to God for healing. The breakup brought me to a place of trust and surrender by forcing something out of my hands that I had hoped to control. I look back and see God's presence and provision.

## A LIFETIME OF LEARNING

When Grant sat down with my parents and asked them for permission to marry me, my parents responded that for them to say yes, he had to commit to doing three things: pursue, provide, and protect. They wanted him to *pursue* me even when it's hard or inconvenient or when he doesn't feel like it. They encouraged him to always date me even after we got married. They challenged him to *provide* for me spiritually, physically, financially, and emotionally. Although he isn't responsible for my contentment and happiness, as the spiritual leader he is responsible for providing. And they challenged him to always *protect* me. Protect my heart, my mind, my body, and our marriage. Grant agreed to pursue, provide, and protect. My dad gave the blessing.

As I mentioned earlier, I knew after my first date with Grant that he was my lifetime. The first date felt like a movie. I came home feeling invincible and on cloud nine. I journaled about how happy I was and that I had met the love of my life. But our relationship wasn't always easy. The next day we went on our second date, and it was hard and confusing. Because of

Grant's anxious thoughts and my own insecurities, we just didn't click. I left the date crying and asking God why he was sending me mixed messages. Then Grant opened up and shared what he was going through, and it made me feel safe and comfortable to share my own struggles with him too. We got through that, but throughout our relationship, there have been a lot of highs and lows. Finding your person doesn't mean it will always be easy and seamless. Lifetime relationships will require a lot of learning, growing, and continually working on the relationship.

I get asked all the time, "How do you know if he's the one? How do you know if he's your lifetime?" I don't know if I have the perfect answer. But I will say I was always led by peace in my decisions—whether that peace closed the door or led me through it. I also have learned throughout my life not to choose the better guy but instead to choose the guy who makes me a better girl. Not someone who just checks off boxes, but someone who loves, serves, and leads me in a way that makes my life more fruitful and fulfilling, my relationship with God better and stronger, my relationships with my friends deeper and more intentional, and my relationship with myself healthier. Grant is that for me.

> *I also have learned throughout my life not to choose the better guy but instead to choose the guy who makes me a better girl.*

But the most important relationship is our relationship with Jesus. Even if you're single and wishing you could find your lifetime man, I encourage you with this: You already have! Jesus is enough and the only one who will never let you down, leave you, or forsake you. He is perfect and consistent. The best lifetime you will ever find. Once I made that relationship my highest priority and the greatest treasure of my heart, everything else fell into place. My relationship with myself grew stronger. My relationships with others became healthier. So, if your highest priority is finding your lifetime human, you will continue to be let down and discontent. Your relationships will continue to suffer because you will be seeking something that ultimately can be found only in a Savior.

I've realized that Grant can't give me everything I want and need. Grant will fail me and let me down (and I will let him down plenty too!). He is the person I have chosen to commit to, and in him I've found my lifetime partner. However, if, before meeting him, I had been in a place of striving and seeking, desperately looking for someone to fill that role, I truly believe our relationship would have failed or it would be unhealthy and toxic. If either of us were hoping for the other person to take the role of God in our hearts, we would be living every day frustrated and discouraged. What makes our relationship so good and so special is that we don't *need* each other; we *want* each other. We don't have to have each other, but we choose each other and commit. I'm thankful we both realize that although we've been given the gift of being each other's lifetime companion, our biggest responsibility and joy is pushing each other closer to our real lifetime partner, Jesus.

A lifetime relationship is a gift from God. Cherish it. This is the relationship you're blessed to have until one of you takes your last breath. Don't get me wrong: Just because it's God-sent doesn't mean it's always going to be easy breezy. All relationships take effort on both parts.

Think about the people in your life over the years, and define those relationships' purposes in your journey. Whether they were there for a reason, a season, or a lifetime, accept that they were meant to be part of your life. See each terminated relationship not as a devastating loss but as a stepping stone. View each heartache and disappointment as another necessary step toward that lifetime relationship. Now that I've found my husband, I can say confidently that every reason or season relationship led me here. And I'd go through them a thousand times over again to find the lifetime love I have today.

We were created by Love, in love, and for love.

—TIM TEBOW, *Shaken*

## BONUS CONTENT

Using your smartphone,
scan the code for bonus content.

waterbrookmultnomah.com/the-love
-everybody-wants-chapter-13-bonus-content

# 14

## MARRIAGE MATERIAL
### Patterns and Purpose Bring Peace

*How do I know if he's the one?*

*He'll be different with me, right?*

*How do I know if I have peace about a relationship?*

So far in this book we've covered how to align our hearts with what God wants, how to heal from and deal with our past, and how to love ourselves. If we do that, we will already have so much of the love everybody wants—even without a guy! We will be fulfilled, secure, and confident in our identity. *Now* it's time to talk about what we should look for in a potential spouse.

Many people base their relationships on passion or potential. But passion can take you only so far. When times are tough, good looks aren't enough. No, when life gets hard, good looks aren't going to save the day. (Not to mention, looks don't last.) When life throws its biggest punches, you don't need someone who can turn you on; you need someone you can lean on. You need someone who is going to be a rock for you—consistent, faithful, and selfless. You need someone who can hold you, pray over you, stick by your side, lead you well, and put you on their back when you're too tired to take another step. I know we talked a little bit about chemistry earlier, and that is important. However, when you're considering marrying someone, physical attraction shouldn't be the main attraction.

And someone may never live up to their potential. When life gets tough, you don't want to have to cling to "one day" or "hopefully it will change." We talked about this in chapter 6. You want to be able to stand in confidence and gratitude, saying, "Only God! Only God could have brought someone like this who I can count on and who pursues me and loves me like Jesus." You don't marry someone for who you hope they will be; you marry someone for who they are right now.

> *You don't marry someone for who you hope they will be; you marry someone for who they are right now.*

In order for us to have a love that lasts, we have to know what we're looking for. You can't score without a goal. You can't shoot without a target. We have to know what we're looking for, or else we will repeat the same cycle over and over again. I like how John C. Maxwell explained this in his book *Intentional Living:* "Most people miss opportunities in life, not because the opportunity wasn't there, but because they didn't have a clue what it looked like when it arrived. They never took the time to figure out what they were looking for. It's all about intentionality. You have to know what you're looking for if you want to find it."[1] Don't settle for "good enough" because you never took the time to pray and figure out what you need and what you're looking for.

I went out with some friends one night to a field to watch a meteor shower. No one will ever accuse me of being obsessed with astronomy, so I wasn't sure what we were looking for. Someone played some music and we roasted marshmallows. It was beautiful out, and we were all just enjoying one another's company. When everyone started packing up, I looked around.

"Where are we going?" I asked.

"Home," my friend responded. I guess I looked confused, because she added, "Madi, the meteor shower is over."

I had missed the entire thing because I had no clue what I was looking for.

For a while, this was me in my relationships. I reasoned, *Oh, he is cute!* Or, *Oh, he opened my door—what a gentleman!* Or, of course, my go-to: *Oh, he must love God since he wore a cross necklace and has a Bible verse in his social media bio!* For a long time, I found myself in one failed relationship after another, mainly because I didn't know what I was really looking for.


## THE THREE P'S

One day in my early twenties, I decided to write out exactly what I needed from a man or, better yet, my husband. I call it the three P's. These are the three things I looked for when I was in a relationship with someone and was trying to decide if he could be the man for the job. It was also a good check for myself to make sure I stayed marriage material! I can't expect what I'm not willing to give.

## 1. Patterns

One of the ways some teachers evaluate incoming kindergartners is to hand them a bag of colored blocks—yellow stars, green squares, red triangles. They ask the student to create different patterns using the shapes. And you know what? These four- and five-year-olds figure it out! But when we become adults, patterns seem to become less obvious to us. A guy who has cheated on his last three girlfriends cheats on us and we act shocked. Maybe we've lost the skill of observing patterns . . . or maybe we'd just rather ignore them and hope we can be the pattern breaker.

Instead, we should take the time to evaluate the habits of the person we are dating. What is he consistently doing? Does he have healthy and godly patterns? Is he consistent in the way he loves you and leads you, even on bad days?

One of the biggest reasons I was so confident that Grant was to be my husband was that I saw the patterns in his life. The way he loved God. The way he loved people. The way he treated me. In private. In public. Consistently. Repeatedly. And for me with my trust issues, this was a big deal. I couldn't leave it up to chance—I needed concrete proof that he was who he said he was. And I couldn't trust the inconsistency of passion and emotion. I needed a man with godly patterns that I could trust and believe in.

I prayed for a man I would be willing to follow, someone whose patterns would challenge me and make me better. And

Grant was exactly that. Was he perfect? No. But we're not looking for perfect patterns. No one has that. We're looking for healthy and holy patterns.

Let's get practical when it comes to evaluating patterns. Maybe ask the questions, How does he steward responsibilities? Time? Money? Relationships? How does he serve others? Or is he only looking to be served? Does he tithe? Does he give back? Does he set an example in his conduct? The truth is, if you see inconsistency in dating, there is a 99 percent chance of that continuing when you're married. As the saying goes, "Past performance is the best indicator of future performance." You want a track record of faithfulness!

In *Intentional Living,* John C. Maxwell put it this way: "When partnering with people, don't choose based on what they *say* they can do, or based on what they did *once*. Choose based on their regular behaviors. That's what tells you what their values are. Too often our choices are made by what we *could* or think we *should* do rather than what we *usually* do. We are all human, so we should give everyone the benefit of the doubt. But we also need to be realistic. We need to have a picture of what we're shooting for."[2]

After two months of dating, Grant and I decided to go on a mission trip to a small, disadvantaged community in the Bahamas to serve and love on the kids there. Watching Grant play basketball with the kids and tell them how much Jesus loves them did something to my heart. Hearing him speak to other young adults on the trip, encouraging them and praying for them, inspired me and touched me in a way I had never experienced. The trip was special because I have such a heart for kids who have been abused or neglected or who are in need. So, watching Grant love those kids told me everything I needed to know about his patterns. But it didn't stop there.

Grant and I were going straight from the Bahamas to see my family in Auburn. At the airport, we ordered an Uber. When we got in the Uber, Grant immediately started making conversation with the driver. The driver opened up about his life and his past. Grant began sharing his testimony and how Jesus changed his life. When we got to my parents' house, Grant prayed over the guy, and he accepted Jesus. It was one of the best experiences of my life. Grant loves people better than I had ever seen.

That week showed me that his life produced good fruit— that he had healthy and holy patterns. And I continued evaluating this throughout our relationship. And each day, each week, each month, I watched Grant consistently pursue what matters most.

## 2. Purpose

Have you ever asked yourself these questions: *Why on earth am I alive? Why was I created? What's so special about me? What am I supposed to do with my life?*

I know I have. Wanna know how many times I changed my major? Yeah, a whopping four times. I was trying to figure out the answer to those questions. I hoped that someone would just show up and tell me my specific calling and mission! Like in *Avengers* movies. I knew I was called to help people and love people but struggled with the *how*.

The Hulk has his crazy strength. Spider-Man has his sticky

webs. Iron Man has his awesome technology and ability to fly. So then, what was my "superpower"? What was my irreplaceable role in God's story?

I usually describe purpose this way:

what you're really passionate about + what you're really good at = your purpose

Once you discover why you were created, you will want to do life with someone whose purpose aligns with yours, even if it's not the same as yours. You need someone who can come alongside you and help you accomplish your purpose, and vice versa.

A verse I think of as a theme for my life is Acts 20:24: "I consider my life worth nothing to me; my only aim is to finish the race and complete the task the Lord Jesus has given me— the task of testifying to the good news of God's grace." It reminds me that my life is bigger than me. I want to live every day of my life on mission. I want to live every day focused on loving God and loving people. I want to live every day committed to joyfully telling people about God's love and grace. I need to be with someone who lives with that same vision for their life. It's impossible to have a healthy and lasting partnership with someone whose purpose and mission don't align with yours.

> It's impossible to have a healthy and lasting partnership with someone whose purpose and mission don't align with yours.

I think about my basketball team in high school. My gift set wasn't the same as the tall girls on my team who could rebound the basketball because they were inches from the backboard. Nor was my gift to catch the ball and shoot it. My gift was to handle the ball and call out plays, to get the ball to the right player at the right time or to make a move and score. I wasn't the best shooter or the best rebounder. But I was really good at dribbling and getting the ball down the court and in the hands of an open player to score a basket. The point is, we were all focused on the same mission: winning the game! But we each had our own specific purpose on the team. And we encouraged, affirmed, and pushed one another in our purposes. That mindset and understanding made each of us better players and teammates.

That's what I believe marriage should look like—two people with different gifts and purposes but the same mission.

Grant's mission is to bring the hope of Jesus to a lost and hurting world. His mission is to love God and love people. So is mine. We share that. And that's important. If we didn't share that, we wouldn't be married. But to take it a step further, Grant and I encourage each other in our unique, God-given purposes. He feels called to minister to athletes and to work with business leaders and pastors. He is more naturally gifted at evangelism and encouragement, leading others with joy and compassion. I feel called to minister to young women struggling with their worth and confidence and to help children that have been abused or abandoned. I'm more naturally gifted at calling others higher by challenging them with God's truth. Together, we love others with grace and truth, with compassion and conviction. We have different gifts and purposes, but they complement one another. They work together.

Proverbs 29:18 says, "Where there is no vision, the people

perish" (KJV). You have to have vision, and it has to be an aligned vision. You can't move forward if you don't know where you're going.

## 3. Peace

When people ask me why I went on reality TV, I respond, "The peace of God." When people ask me why I moved to Dallas and away from my family, I respond, "The peace of God." When people ask me why I married Grant and how I knew he was the man for me, I respond, "The peace of God." I'm so confident in all those decisions, some of the most pivotal decisions of my life, because of the peace God gave me.

The Bible says in Isaiah 55:12,

> You will go out in joy
> and be led forth in peace;
> the mountains and hills
> will burst into song before you,
> and all the trees of the field
> will clap their hands.

For a lot of us, being led by peace sounds wonderful. But practically speaking, we have no idea what that would even look like. If we are called to be led by peace, we first have to know what peace even is. Is it a feeling? A moment? Something written in the sky? Is it available to some and not others?

You might hear the word *peace* and think of pedicures and spa treatments. Or a clean and quiet house. Maybe a nice drive somewhere scenic. While those forms of peace are certainly nice, they're not the kind of peace I'm talking about, because they're temporary. You'll chip your nails. Your house will get dirty. And inevitably, you'll hit traffic.

Peace from the world is attainable only in certain environments and is contingent on certain circumstances. And it's not a bad thing! But it's not the *best* thing either. The peace God gives is not of this world. It's not contingent on your season of life, upbringing, financial situation, or effort and performance. God's peace is everlasting. It's not a peace you find in a warm bath; it's an inward peace that can't be taken. A peace that rests in security, not emotions.

When you're making a decision and feel an uneasy restlessness inside you, *that's* the absence of God's peace. See, there is God's will—which is walking in his perfect peace. Then there is self-will—which is walking in, well, whatever we want to walk in. You know peace only when you know him. The more you know him, the more you know his voice, the more you know his heart, the more you'll have his peace.

Peace can be a difficult topic to unpack because it's spiritual. It's not a law you can follow or an emotion you can feel. Only in intimately walking with Christ and knowing the Spirit of God can you know peace—what it feels like, what it sounds like, what it looks like.

John 16:33 says, "I have told you these things, so that in me you may have peace. In this world you will have trouble. But take heart! I have overcome the world."

Peace is an integral aspect of God's personality. It's who he is. So if we need more of it, we need more of him.

*Okay,* you're probably thinking. *This sounds great, Madi. But I need more specifics.* I got you. While peace *is* spiritual, you can take certain steps to pursue it.

Here are three ways I walk in the peace of God:

1. **Prayer: What does God speak to you?** Matthew 6:33 tells us to seek first the kingdom of God and that everything else will be given to us. If God is peace, then the closer I get to God, the closer I get to peace. One of the most effective ways to get closer to God is through prayer.

   The *only* way anyone would be able to explain my ending a four-year relationship with someone I thought I wanted to marry is that I prayed. I sought the will of God for my life. And he spoke. He led me. He showed me—through prayer.

   On the exterior, the relationship made sense. He was a great guy who loved God. But when I prayed about our future together, I always experienced a restless uneasiness. Looking back, I can see clearly why God didn't bring peace about us ending up together. First of all, Grant. And second, I wouldn't have fulfilled my purpose or mission by staying in that relationship.

2. **Truth: What does God's Word say?** When I'm seeking the peace of God, I'll often turn to his Word in decision-making. After I wrestle in prayer with God, the next step is to make sure that my choices and my motives line up with his Word. If my will doesn't line up with God's Word, I know that I'm operating out of my own desires and not God's. I know that if I continue down that path, I won't find peace.

3. **Community and accountability: What do others feel?** When you're concerned about something in your life, run your concerns by your closest and most trusted friends. But be very careful with this one. People are not God. God can, however, speak through people who love and know him.

Once, I was in a relationship that I didn't have peace about, but I really wanted it to work. The people around me kept telling me they didn't feel this was God's best, and they were concerned for me. Eventually my mentor looked at me and said, "End the relationship now. If you don't, you will not be all God has called you to be."

I finally ended it, but it took more than six months of the closest people around me warning me and praying for me and challenging me to end the relationship.

Yet, in another way, the wrong community can cause more confusion and even lead you to make an unwise decision. There were moments in dating Grant that I confided in the wrong people with frustrations or concerns. The advice they gave me contradicted what the Spirit of peace and truth had already spoken to me. If I had taken their advice, Grant and I wouldn't be married today.

This is where you have to use discernment. You can't just do what your girlfriends say you should do without praying about it and searching God's Word *first*. Then I would suggest confiding in two or three people who have strong relationships with Jesus and whose lives look the way you'd like your life to look one day.

When it comes to peace in your relationship, there are certain questions you should also ask yourself. How do you feel when he's around? When he's not around? Do you trust his relationship with Jesus as much as your own? Does he bring you a sense of security? Does his decision-making bring you security? Does his self-control bring you security? Does his integrity bring you security? How do those closest to you feel about him?

When the relationship is from God, there's a supernatural peace. When it's not from God, there's doubt, confusion, uneasiness, justification, excuses. When you talk about your man, do you feel like you have to defend why you are with him? Do you find yourself anxious when he doesn't text back for hours? When he's apart from you, are you afraid of what decisions he might make?

> When the relationship is from God, there's a supernatural peace. When it's not from God, there's doubt, confusion, uneasiness, justification, excuses.

I've been in relationships when all the right boxes were checked but I lacked peace. To everyone else, we were the perfect couple and breaking up sounded ridiculous. But somewhere deep within me there was a small hesitation, a little doubt, and a thought like, *Is this really God's best for me?* It's easy to ignore that check in your spirit, the lack of peace deep within, and to keep carrying on. And I'm not saying that you won't get peace later. However, one of the worst things you could do is commit to a forever with someone if you have a lack of peace. When people ask me if I had the experience of

"When you know, you know," I always answer yes because there was peace from day one. And peace is always your answer.

But I want you to understand that peace doesn't mean perfect. When you find someone who is marriage material, there will likely be some speed bumps and hard days and conflict. Peace doesn't mean it's easy. There were many moments it would have been easier for me to walk away from Grant than to stay in a relationship with him. And I know he would say the same about me. We both had to overcome a lot to make our relationship work: my trust issues, his anxiety, my world of social media and reality TV, insecurities, fear—you name it! There were a lot of moments one of us wanted to walk away, but God kept giving us peace for the relationship and grace for the other person.

Like we've said, peace isn't an emotion. A lot of people stay in relationships they shouldn't be in and argue that they just have peace. Peace doesn't mean that the relationship makes you feel good and that it's easy and comfortable. Peace is contentment and confidence. Peace is when there is a divine flow to the relationship you can't explain.

*Peace isn't an emotion.*

With Grant, I trusted his relationship with God. I watched as he loved, served, and prioritized that relationship over everything else. He was fully surrendered to God. I trusted his words and commitments because he followed through with action. I trusted his humility and authenticity because he was willing to admit when he was wrong and he was always willing to grow. I felt safe and secure with him because he respected and honored me, alone and in front of others. I felt so much rest when

I was with him, like the little kid inside me came out in full joy and innocence. I had so much peace because being in a relationship with him made me want to get closer to God. When we were together, I felt God's presence. When we weren't together, I would hit my knees and thank God for bringing me a man like him. He made me better. And he was the first man I had ever dated that I fully respected. When you have peace about someone or something, there is a level of rest and trust.

To have the love everybody wants, we have to have peace.

> The peace of God, which transcends all
> understanding, will guard your hearts and your
> minds in Christ Jesus.
>
> —Philippians 4:7

## BONUS CONTENT

Using your smartphone,
scan the code for bonus content.

waterbrookmultnomah.com/the-love
-everybody-wants-chapter-14-bonus-content

# 15

## WORTH THE WAIT

### Embracing What's Already Yours

> How long do I have to wait?
> How can I find the love that is already mine?
> Will it be worth it?

One time I jumped on a stranger's back in the middle of Target.

Have you ever accidentally waved at someone, thinking they were someone else, but it turned out that it was *not* the person you thought it was? Yeah, this used to happen to me a lot because I had terrible vision and refused to wear contacts because they hurt my eyes. (Like I mentioned earlier, I got Lasik and now have perfect vision.) There was this one time, though, that was much worse than the occasional wave or high five to some stranger.

I was walking in Target one summer, shopping for who knows what, and I saw one of my high school friends in the distance. I yelled her name, and she didn't turn around, so I thought, *I'll just jump on her back and scare her!* A logical thought, right? When I was in midair, about to land on her back, I realized she was not, in fact, my high school friend. No, she was a random girl who just *looked like* my high school friend.

By that point, it was too late to stop. I was already on her back. This poor girl threw me off, shooting me a look of shock and disgust. Which, honestly, I deserved.

Not knowing what else to do, I smiled and said, "Have a nice day!" and darted off.

I know. I'm *that* weird girl in the local Target.

If I had just waited *five more seconds* before acting, I could have spared both of us the embarrassment of that experience. But I didn't wait. Instead, I moved impulsively, without having full knowledge of the situation. In looking back at my life, I can see how not waiting could have easily become a pattern for me.

Take, for instance, this job I had once that I absolutely hated. I was there for only eight months, but at the time it felt like eight years. I was anxious every day; I cried before going into the office; I dreaded Monday mornings. I didn't even feel like myself anymore. Everything in my life was being affected because of how much I was struggling with this job. I felt that impulse to quit and figure out finances later. Anything seemed to be a better option than sitting and waiting.

But I had learned by that point—through *not* waiting and paying for it later—that sometimes the waiting is the point. The waiting is what gets you ready. The waiting holds you until it's *God's* time for there to be a change. So instead of handing in my notice, I got on my knees. I started praying for the Lord to just place something new in front of me, because I didn't even know where I wanted to go from there. But for months, I heard nothing but silence. It felt like I was walking down a pitch-black tunnel without a glimmer of light at the end.

Now that I'm on the other side of that experience, I can see the Lord's hand in all of it. That job wasn't right for me or for my wiring. But I learned more about myself and my skills and career goals than I would have ever learned otherwise. During the waiting, God was still faithful. He sustained me. He helped me keep going. And he provided a way out when the timing was right. And when I think about where I am now in my career, I'm a thousand times happier and feel full of joy and purpose.

If I had to go through all of that to get here, I would do it all over again. The Lord proves to be the faithful God he promises that he is, even when we don't see the light at the end of the tunnel. Sometimes we have to endure hard, dry seasons to get to the life-giving, fruitful seasons. But like all things in life that are worthy of our hearts, it's been so worth the wait.

## ON DEMAND

What's your favorite show to watch? I'm not a huge TV person, but when I have time to watch, I love *Fixer Upper*. I feel like it's been around forever. But you know what I *won't* watch? Any TV show where you have to wait an entire week for a new episode to come out. I can't stand it—the speculating, the wondering, the waiting. Since I can remember, there's been either DVR or streaming services, so I'm not used to having to wait.

If you're reading this, there's a good chance you've also grown up in this on-demand generation that's accustomed to getting what we want when we want it. We have literally every question's answer at our fingertips. We can have our groceries and meals delivered. We can get therapy and seek medical advice online. We can even skip lines using different apps on our phones. There's so little we actually have to wait on these days. I think that's one of the reasons so many of us struggle with waiting—we're not used to it. It feels like a loss of the control we're familiar with.

But you can admit that some things are worth waiting for. Right? You wouldn't eat chicken before it's been thoroughly cooked. You wouldn't leave the doctor's office before getting your test results. You would even add your name to the waiting list at a restaurant where you really wanted to eat. Waiting for what we want isn't common in our culture, but when we think it's worth it, we're willing to wait.

> Waiting for what we want isn't common in our culture, but when we think it's worth it, we're willing to wait.

Let me ask you a question: Aren't *you* worth the wait? Your full becoming? Your character's development? God's perfect plan for you? Your future? All those things are *well* worth a little delayed gratification. Because, in the waiting, we aren't just waiting. We're growing. We're being prepared for what comes next. And *who* comes next.

I started off this book saying it wasn't a manual for how to get a boyfriend or a manifesto that you have to be in a relationship to have a meaningful life. While we may long to find someone to spend our lives with, our deeper desire should be to become the people we would hope to find out there in the world—people who love God and love themselves. People of conviction, purpose, and peace.

In this final chapter, I want to recap what I hope you take away from this book—that there is a better way to approach the desire for love that is hardwired in our hearts. And it's this: We must look to God first and learn to see ourselves as he sees us, and only then will we be ready to love whoever God brings into our lives.

Yes, you may have to wait longer than you feel comfortable for God to move, but he isn't bothered by our discomfort. He knows that we grow when we're out of our comfort zone and forced to fully rely on him. During our times of waiting, it's up to us to do the practical work and trust God to do the supernatural.

Your future is worth waiting for. The person God has for you is worth waiting for. God's plan is worth waiting for. There's a reason his plan isn't an on-demand plan. There's work to be done between where we are and what we want.

> There's work to be done between where we are and what we want.

## DELAYED GRATIFICATION

Have you seen those videos on social media where a parent puts a cupcake on the table in front of their kid and then leaves the room while the camera is still running? Before exiting, they say to their kid, "If you can wait fifteen minutes, when I come back, you can have *two* cupcakes."

Kids are hilarious. Some of them can't deny themselves the sugary goodness, so they dive right in and gobble up whatever's in front of them. Other kids toe the line. They take a tiny nibble, thinking it won't be noticed, or they lick the icing for just a taste. These are my people! And then there are other kids who put their hands in their laps and wait patiently for Mom or Dad to return and reward them with a delicious prize.

This is a practice in our ability to delay gratification. Delayed gratification is a totally foreign concept in our on-demand culture. So many of us are waiting for a partner to walk through life with. Someone we can be teammates with, accomplishing far more together than we ever could alone. But . . . we were made for *more*. More than a life of waiting and dreaming of the day we get married and start a family of our own. More than a life of looking in the rearview mirror and regretting our past and questioning our worth. More than a life of feeling "less than" because we're unattached. More than a life spent settling for the crumbs of love given to us by people who don't see our value.

> What we ultimately want may require us to experience some delayed gratification, but the more we're promised is immeasurably worth the wait.

Yes, what we ultimately want may require us to experience some delayed gratification, but the *more* we're promised is immeasurably worth the wait.


## A LOVE THAT NEVER FAILS

One time I had a voicemail that said I won ten thousand dollars. I'm sure we've all had our own version of this call—Lisa from the warranty department wants to offer a free extension on your car's coverage. The call I'm talking about was a little before the robocallers of today, so I took it seriously! The message said all I needed to do was call that number back and claim my cash prize. I was so excited and followed the steps. As you might imagine, it turned out to be a total scam. A scam that cost me three thousand dollars! I had naïvely given the "company" my bank card information so they could credit my account. I ended up having to cancel the card and felt like a total idiot.

I wanted it all to be true—that I had won ten grand! I wanted it to be true so badly that I was willing to risk giving personal information to a total stranger over the phone. And you're reading this and thinking, *Madi. Seriously?* Yes, seriously. But I'm willing to bet we all do this more often than we think— believe in something that's too good to be true. Especially when it comes to love.

When something sounds too good to be true, it usually is. I think we've all experienced this truth in one way or another. But I also think it's this same truth that holds so many of us back from embracing the relentless love, acceptance, and grace offered to us by God. We think, *Okay. God loves me no matter what? How is that possible? He accepts me despite my sins? He forgives me despite my pride? He wants a relationship with me right where I am, right now? That sounds too good to be true.* So we immediately disqualify ourselves from being eligible for the love God offers all of us freely.

You know what? It *is* too good to be true. But it *is* true. His love is the love everybody wants. And it's already ours. I honestly think if we understood even a fraction of how much God loves us, we wouldn't hesitate to drop everything that distracts us from him and serve him wildly. See, we can't measure the love of God with the same tools we use to measure the love of a human. Because God isn't human. He doesn't love with the heart of a human; he loves with the heart of God—the creator of love.

> I honestly think if we understood even a fraction of how much God loves us, we wouldn't hesitate to drop everything that distracts us from him and serve him wildly.

Maybe you've heard the saying "There is a God-shaped hole in your heart." As strange as that may be to imagine and as overused as that saying may be, that's really how it works. We were made for *more*. And it doesn't get any *more* than the endless love of our Creator. It's his love that completes us. Nothing else and no one else can fill the space in our hearts and lives that God is meant to fill.

Want to know how I'm confident of this? Think about it: How many married people do you know who are still unhappy? My guess is more than one. That's because marriage alone doesn't completely satisfy us—only God can do that.

Once we learn to accept the love that is so generously offered to us by God, we can take the next step in our journey to wholeness: loving ourselves.

## ME, MYSELF, AND I

If you were to rate how much you like yourself on a scale from 0 to 10, where would you fall? I'm not talking about your bad days, when even your hair on the "good side" won't cooperate. I'm talking about your general feelings toward yourself. If you have to pause for longer than a few beats to think about your answer, you might have some work to do.

Another way to gauge your relationship with yourself is to think about this: How comfortable are you with yourself? I know we all have insecurities and things we'd like to change about ourselves. I'm talking about overall—how do you *really* feel about yourself? When you look in the mirror, what do you see? Do you only ever see your imperfections? Can you ever compliment your appearance? When you get asked in an interview what your strengths are, what comes to mind? Anything? Or when you take photos with friends, do you let them post only the photos you've edited and filtered?

The best way I've found to work on how I feel about myself is to constantly remind myself what God says about me. I write down verses like "Because you belong to Christ, you have been made complete" (Colossians 2:10, NIRV) and "We are God's handiwork, created in Christ Jesus to do good works, which God prepared in advance for us to do" (Ephesians

2:10). If you're not familiar with the Bible, just do an internet search for "what God thinks about me." You can set reminders on your phone to read these verses, absorbing them as you rehearse them over and over.

The other way I've found to grow in self-acceptance is to pay attention to my own thoughts about myself. If we were to say out loud everything we thought, how often would we be saying hurtful things about ourselves? Over time, the way we feel about ourselves will become the way we allow others to treat us.

For the next thirty days, I challenge you to put out a jar and put a dollar in it every time you have a negative thought about yourself or say something negative about yourself. When it's full, donate it to charity. You may be broke by the end of the month, but hopefully you'll like yourself a lot more!

> *Over time, the way we feel about ourselves will become the way we allow others to treat us.*

Loving God and accepting his unconditional love for you is the *only* way to be certain that you're becoming the person you and God want you to be for your future spouse. Let me explain it this way. I try to eat very healthy. I like the way my body feels when I'm eating foods that are good and life-giving. But a few weeks ago, I stopped at the grocery store for the first time in a while. And I was *starving.* I grabbed a quick dinner on the way home and then immediately unpacked my groceries.

When I looked at all I had bought, I was genuinely shocked by some of my choices: sugary cereal, a package of cookies from the bakery, and white powder donuts—just to name a few. *Who bought all this stuff?* It was like I had blacked out and thrown everything that looked halfway decent into my cart in a blind hunger craze. When we try dating before we've set our hearts right with God and ourselves, it's like grocery shopping on an empty stomach. Our standards are lower, we're willing to settle, and the result is often shocking and embarrassing.

## THE RIGHT RELATIONSHIP

Once you've learned to love God and love yourself, you've given yourself the best possible foundation to build the *right* relationship. And how will you know it's right?

The right relationship won't make you feel that you've settled for less.

The right relationship won't make you insecure, and you won't get the feeling that something is missing.

The right relationship will improve your sense of self-worth. You will feel affirmed and secure.

The right relationship will push you toward pursuing your purpose.

The right relationship won't require a compromise of your values, morals, or faith.

The right relationship will bring out your best qualities. You will feel a strong discomfort just by thinking about mediocrity. When you are in the relationship you were destined to be in, you will always find new inspiration to become the best version of yourself. You will always want to improve, because you know that your relationship deserves the best.

And most importantly, the right relationship will draw you closer to Jesus.

## THE BIG DAY

Today is October 29, 2022. It's the day I've been preparing for my entire life. Today is my wedding day.

On this day I will enter into an irrevocable covenant with the man God has purposed for me. I will take his hand and his name, and together we will fulfill what we believe to be God's perfect will for our lives. There are ten thousand things happening at once as I write this, but I felt compelled to pause and soak up the scene around me.

When I think about the difficult experiences that litter the path behind me—the broken promises, the unrealized dreams, the hurts, the growing pains, and the waiting—I can tell you with absolute confidence that I'd go through it all again to be where I am right now. Actually, I'd go through it all again and again and again. Because I'm certain that I'm exactly where God wants me to be. And as in love with Grant as I am, it's *that* thought that brings me deep peace and overflowing joy!

When I look around me, I see the people who held me in the waiting.

I've got my wonderful parents here—the ones who raised me and taught me how to love Jesus. They also demonstrated to me how a husband and wife should treat each other. My parents aren't perfect, but I've never once seen them be disrespectful or unloving to the other. I've got my sisters—my best friends—who were my safe place and biggest support system. They cried with me and laughed with me through all of life's twists and turns. I've got my gorgeous girlfriends in their dresses by my side, getting their hair Texas-high and their eyelashes waterproofed. I know when I walk down the aisle, I'll see the faces of pastors and mentors and small-group leaders who have helped build my faith and loaned me their strength when mine felt inadequate.

Yes, today I will become Madison Prewett Troutt. I will enter into the most important earthly relationship I will ever have—but it was never meant to be the *only* relationship I will ever have. I'm so thankful I didn't spend the waiting *waiting*. I'm grateful that I spent the waiting *preparing*. I spent the waiting working on myself, working on my relationship with God, and working on my relationships with others.

God's commandments to us in Matthew 22:34–40 are clear. The greatest commandments—the most important guides and safeguards you can have in place to preserve your life and future—are simple: Love God, and love others as yourself. If we can do this in the waiting, the waiting won't be waiting at all. It will be building, growing, and preparing.

I'll put on my veil a little later. It's beautiful—breathtaking! I had it embroidered with the words "Worth the wait," because what Grant and I share has been. But not only has the wait been worth it; it's also helped me become worthy of the calling of being a godly wife—it's helped me become ready. I'm building this marriage with Grant on the solid foundation of the love everybody wants: the love of Christ. The love that existed before I did, and the love that will persist long after I've left this earth.

In praying about how I would finish this book, I had the idea of sharing the vows I will say to Grant today. I hope you hear echoes of God's faithfulness and love throughout these words, whispered from his heart to yours.

My Love,

On December 3, a miracle happened. I met you. I knew on our first date that you would be my forever. Every prayer I had prayed. Every list I had made. Every detail. It was you.

And I realized that night . . .

I chose you before I knew you.

I sacrificed for you before I met you.

I fought for you before I found you.

I waited well for you. I prayed hard for you.

You were worth it.

You were worth the pain and tears when I didn't understand God's plan.

You were worth the lonely nights.

You were worth the long seasons of waiting and longing.

You exceeded my biggest and boldest prayers.

You are everything I always wanted and exactly what I needed.

A strong leader with a servant's heart. A man of bold faith. A joyful and charismatic spirit. A man after God's own heart.

And a man I am proud of and proud to be his. Each day with you, I become more and more of who I was created to be.

I know I have found the one my soul loves. So now have all of me. Body, soul, and spirit. I am yours. I have saved it all for you. And I promise and commit to keep it yours. To honor you and respect you. To follow you and submit to you. To love you. Always. No matter what.

When it's hard. When I don't want to. I vow to fight for you. To fight for us. I vow to make you my second greatest priority, only behind loving and serving God with all my heart. I vow to stand by you in your highest highs and lowest lows.

I vow to never stop laughing and dancing with you, driving around downtown, blaring music and getting lost and hitting curbs.

I vow to affirm you and remind you of who you are when you forget. I vow to believe our love will never fail, because God's love has never and will never fail us.

Grant Michael Troutt, I know I was made for loving you. God knew exactly what he was doing. When he created you, he had to have been thinking about me. You were so worth the wait.

## BONUS CONTENT

Using your smartphone,
scan the code for bonus content.

waterbrookmultnomah.com/the-love
-everybody-wants-chapter-15-bonus-content

# Bonus Chapter

## THE LOVE HE WANTS

by Grant Troutt

What's up, everybody? It's your boy, Grant Troutt! The better half. Kidding! Well, kind of . . . Let me just say it's good to be here. How did I end up in this book? Honestly, I'm just as surprised as you are. But here I am.

If you've made it to this chapter, you've already experienced a *glimpse* of the most beautiful heart in the entire world—Madi Rose. Isn't she incredible? I can't believe that by the time this book is in your hands, we'll have been married more than two years. I love her so much! Her smile, her joy, her shoe game, her heart for Jesus, her weird baby voice . . . *Okay, focus, Grant!*

I remember when Madi asked me to read this book before it was even published, when it was just a rough draft on her computer. As I read, tears began to stream down my face because I've seen firsthand her love for God and for you. Yes, *you*. You've been prayed for and believed in. Not only by Madi, but more importantly by an all-powerful, all-knowing God. This is the single most important truth you'll take away from this book: God loves you. And *this* is the love that changes everything.

As you now know, there's an order to love when it comes to relationships. God's love is the foundation of all others. His is the love you were made from and made for. If you don't know him, if you don't know why you were created, you'll never get other relationships right. After all, we can love as we were created to only if we are connected to the true and main source of love—God.

## WHAT WAS I MADE FOR?

If we're honest, we all want to feel seen, known, and loved. It's at the core of every single human being walking this planet. But if we look to the world and its offerings to fulfill this need, we'll be disappointed and discontent. Despite having versions of love all around us—rom-coms, social media, love songs, and so on—something is missing. Something isn't working.

Although we have access to connection, most of us would say we feel lonely, disconnected, and unknown. Millennials and Gen Zers have been described as the loneliest and most disconnected generations ever.[1] We've never had more access to resources on the topic of dating and relationships than we do now, like podcasts on relationships, books about love, articles on how to find the one, apps for dating, even reality TV shows where the couple gets engaged after knowing each other for only six weeks. (Who would ever do something like that? *I'm kidding!*) So we think, *I need to find a significant other in order to feel less lonely.* Or, *Once I'm married, I'll be happy.* That is the lie we believe. Clearly something isn't working.

But what if, instead of turning to culture for the standard and definition of love, we went to the Creator of it? The One who created marriage and the idea of relationships in the first place. The Author of love—*Love itself*!

To figure out the complexities around dating and marriage and the whole purpose of it all, we must first know why we exist. We need to answer these questions: *Who am I? Why am I here? What was I made for?*

To find the answers, let's go back to the beginning. The Bible says in Genesis 1:27 that you and I have been created by God in his image: "God created man in his own image, in the image of God he created him; male and female he created them" (ESV). To make it simple, we were created by God and for God. So, who are you? *You are an image bearer.* Why are you here? *To reflect that image to the world, sort of like the moon.* Wait— let me explain what I mean by that.

One of the things Madi and I like to do is to go out and look at the night sky. How romantic, right? One night we were sitting outside observing the way the moon lit up the whole sky. Did you know that the moon cannot give off *any* light in and of itself? None. Only when it reflects the light of the sun can it give off any light! How crazy? As I thought about the way the moon reflects the sun's light, God spoke to my heart, saying, "That is you." The only light *we* have to give is when the Son of God shines in us and through us. In and of ourselves, we don't have any light to give the world. Just as the moon reflects the sun's light to brighten a dark sky, we can reflect the Son (Jesus) to light up a dark world. So, when we position ourselves in relationship with God, we will reflect that love to light up the world.

About four years ago, when I was still a newer believer, I was asked to lead an NBA chapel for a team in Dallas. I'm not sure why they asked me or how they found me. (Maybe they had the wrong Grant? I didn't care. They asked me!) I was excited, passionate, and super nervous. My heart was racing. These professional basketball players were used to hearing from fifty-year-old pastors who could probably recite the entire Bible, and here I came, a twenty-three-year-old who had just gotten saved. I'm pretty sure the only verse I had memorized was John 3:16. But despite being nervous, I was ready! As I shared my testimony and all that God had rescued me from, I could see they were curious and wanted this freedom I had found and was so passionately talking about. I looked at these players—guys who had money, girls, cars, fame . . . everything the world says should bring happiness and purpose and satisfaction—and all I could think was, *Something is missing.* And I understood.

I remember looking into their eyes and asking them, "Has the NBA satisfied your heart like you thought it would when you were in high school?" Heads shook and voices murmured, "No."

I continued, "Ten thousand people are about to cheer and chant your name, but does anybody actually know you? The real you?" The room was silent.

While I'm not an NBA superstar, I've tasted and seen enough of what this world has to offer me, and I've come to believe what the Bible says in Ecclesiastes 3:11: "He has put eternity into man's heart" (ESV). Meaning, nothing of this world will ever be able to satisfy the deepest desires and longings of our hearts. It must be something greater—something out of this world, something eternal. Better yet, *Someone* eternal. When we understand the reason we were created—to know God and to make him known—only then can we understand the purpose of dating and marriage.

## LASTING LOVE: HOW TO BE COMPLETE

When I met Madi—although she was the most beautiful woman I had ever laid eyes on and rocked Jordans like I didn't even know girls could—my eyes were captivated by something much deeper than her body and her style. I knew there was something different about her. And as I continued to date her, I processed questions like, *Is she willing to give up all that is comfortable for the sake of the gospel? Is she sure of her true worth in Christ? Does she have a heart to serve, give, and lay down her life for other people? Is she in community and connected to a local church? How does she treat people who can do nothing for her?* I needed to know that the woman I was evaluating and wanted to marry was someone who was not just beautiful (although I'm not mad at how things turned out) but was sold out for and submitted to Jesus. I wanted to know that she would be someone who would help me love God more and spread his love, not someone who would pull me away from him. Because if the purpose of my life is to know God and make him known, then one of my top priorities in dating and ultimately in marriage was to unite with someone who would help me know God more and make him known more to the world.

As I dated Madi and got to know her and learn her heart, I saw a woman so in love with God. A woman confident in who she was as a daughter of Christ. I was drawn to her joy. Her radical obedience to follow Jesus. Her passion to love people and live a life on purpose. And when people ask me how I knew that she was the one, I answer, "She didn't need me!" *That* is what was the most beautiful thing about her. She knew that she was God's daughter and that he completed her. As Madi said in chapter 5, "a partner in life is meant to complement you, *not* complete you." You and I were created to be fully satisfied in a personal relationship with God. And then we are to give his love to the world around us.

Her confidence came not from anything external but rather from who she believed God was and who he said she was. She had a calm and confident security that whether our relationship worked out or not, her value and calling would be unshaken. She didn't need me; she just wanted me. And that was unbelievably attractive.

And if you are reading this, wondering what all men want, well, I can't speak for all men. I'll just speak from my experience and what I see in the mentors and community around me. The *right* man is looking for a woman who is first and foremost complete and confident in God. That's what I found in Madi. She never tried to fake it with me. She was completely herself. She didn't need me to fill a void in her heart or even tell her who she was (although, since my love language is words of affirmation, I was quick to tell her of her amazing and awesome qualities). It was her faith in God and in who he made her to be that set her apart. That didn't come overnight for her. Moments with God that nobody saw had created the beautiful heart I was being so undeniably drawn to.

So, what do women want in a man? Hopefully, they also want someone who is complete and confident in God. Someone who can lead well because he is led well (by God's Spirit!). But I do know that some women have a list that is more like this: tall, dark, handsome, wealthy but not worldly, confident but not cocky, and more. Yet I can't tell you how many times I've listened to girls talk to Madi, tearfully discussing their single status, when they've overlooked some amazing men who just didn't meet all their requirements. If that's you, maybe you need to ask God in prayer, "Does my list honor you? Is this the type of man you have called me to be with?" Because, at the end of the day, many of those required features will fade. In ten years, when you're sick and the baby is crying and life feels heavy and overwhelming, what type of man do you want by your side? A flashy charmer who still acts like a boy, someone you fear you can't even fully trust? Or a man in love with Jesus and in love with you, who can be a rock when things get hard?

I also want to say, *people attract the type of person they advertise to.*

So, are you more concerned with showing him your heart or your hips? Your care for Jesus or your curves in those jeans? If you gain a man because of your body, I promise that you'll lose him because of it too. And where you look for a spouse matters. The man you want is found not at the club but at the church. Just saying! I know I sound like a preacher, but it's true.

It's also important to know that you can't rely on your own strength to make a relationship work. A few months into our marriage, Madi and I went into a restaurant and a guy in a wheelchair and his girlfriend came up to us and said they followed us on social media and appreciated our relationship. The guy shared his story of how he became wheelchair bound. They had been on vacation and got in a tragic car accident while in their Uber. He was an athlete, healthy and good looking, with his girlfriend of more than four years. And then his life changed forever in a moment. Now he is in a wheelchair for the rest of his life. I looked over as he spoke and noticed his girlfriend had started crying. I could see the pain and confusion and fear in his eyes as I looked back at him. So much had changed between them since their relationship began. "She didn't sign up for this," he said. I imagine he was really wondering, *Is she going to leave me? Will she love me through this?* Finally they looked at Madi and me and asked, "What relationship advice would you give us?"

We sat in silence for a moment, trying not to cry ourselves. Our hearts were hurting for them. I mean, what would you say?

Madi and I looked at them, and I said, "Whether in a

wheelchair or not, in health or in sickness, whether rich or poor, if you try to love him or love her in your own strength, it will never be enough. It will fail and will run out." They looked confused, not expecting that answer. I went on to say, "When you love for any other reason but to serve and sacrifice, that love will run dry. Because feelings run dry."

Then I shared with them a story in the Bible where Jesus found a woman drawing water at a well. She felt hopeless, rejected, overlooked, and burdened, and she had been looking for love in all the wrong places. She had been married five times, and now she was living with a guy who wasn't even her husband. Jesus gazed at her with love and gently said, "I can give you living water that will never run dry. I will give you water that will never leave you thirsty again" (see John 4:14). And in that moment, she realized she had found something that no man could possibly give her. For Jesus is the living water that satisfies us and allows us to love and live in even the hardest of circumstances.

The couple at the restaurant had been through so much, and they were looking at each other to provide the answer to their problems and pain. We reminded them of John 14:6 when Jesus said, "I am the way and the truth and the life." *He* is the only answer. And when we try to love without him, we'll find ourselves weary, burdened, isolated, and confused—but when we make him the foundation of our relationships, no matter the storms that come our way (and they will come—it's a guarantee!), we can have a love that is unshaken, a love that lasts.

I'm not guaranteed a perfectly healthy wife for the rest of

my life. As scary as it is to say that, it's true. If I've learned anything in marriage so far, it's been this: Love isn't a noun; it's a verb. Love isn't something you feel or fall into. It isn't an arrow you are struck with by Cupid. It's a choice you make. A choice to serve and to sacrifice even when it's hard. A choice to pursue, protect, and provide even when it feels impossible. Read 1 Corinthians 13 and see how Paul defined what true love really looks like. It's action, not feeling.

## A LOVE WORTH DYING FOR

Some people are almost embarrassed by their desire for a spouse. I want you to know that this desire isn't bad; it's biblical! God looked at Adam in Genesis 2:18 and said, "It is not good for the man to be alone," and he then created Eve. Even God is relationship—a very unique relationship in himself—as Father, Son, and Holy Spirit. My point is this: *You are hardwired to crave relationship, because you were made for it.*

One caveat, however. Although the desire for a spouse isn't wrong, prioritizing it over a relationship with God is. Marriage isn't the ultimate goal of life. Loving God is. A relationship with a spouse isn't eternal, but a relationship with God is.

Maybe you are thinking, *Well, that's easy for you to say, because you are married!* True. I am married. But I didn't live any less or love God differently when I was single. I lived fully. I lived purposefully. And I want that for you too. Instead of constantly looking to see if your spouse could be around the next corner, seek Jesus with all your heart. Learn the way you are wired and the gifts and passions inside you. Get plugged into a local church and serve. Travel and go on mission trips, serving and helping others in greater need. Memorize Scripture, and soak in the Word of God. Have game nights with your best friends, and stay up late asking one another questions that challenge and encourage your faith and friendship.

The really cool thing about Madi and me is that we weren't looking for each other. (I mean, a blind date . . . Really?) But what I love about our beginning is that we were running in our own lanes. *Both of us were more concerned with loving and glorifying God than being distracted and discontent with our relational status.* Listen, there were hard times for sure. Don't hear me say it was always easy. But we fought for contentment, which is a promise for those in Christ. I know it can feel lonely. I know you see others around you and feel a twinge of longing. But I want you to pray a prayer that changed my life: "Lord, don't deliver me until you've developed me." Trust his timing. Trust his plan. He is doing something in the waiting.

What is married life like? It's both awesome and hard, sometimes simultaneously. We learned quickly that marriage wasn't just endless sleepovers with your best friend. There are bills to be paid, chores to be done, and the endless and daily choice to die to self. John 3:16 tells us how Jesus loved us: He gave his life for us. He died so we could live. He hung on so we could let go. He sacrificed so we could be saved. In 1 John 3:16, we are called to that same kind of love. *Real love is not just worth waiting for but also worth dying for.* This verse says that, because of God's love for us, we ought to love by laying our lives down for one another. So, marriage is death. "That's so intense, Grant!" Yep. And in dying to yourself, you find real life and love. I love Madi even more now than I did on our wedding day because of how much we've sacrificed for each other. Sacrifice cultivates intimacy.

You want to know something really cool? The Bible starts with a wedding and ends with a wedding. The Bible starts with Adam and Eve becoming one and ends with Jesus and his bride (you and me) becoming one. The purpose of marriage is way bigger than what we think. It isn't for our own happiness and satisfaction. It isn't just so we don't have to go through life alone. No, it represents something much bigger than that. Timothy Keller said it this way: "Marriage is designed to make us holy, not happy."[2]

When you understand this, you recognize the significance of the person and way in which you date. Your question goes from "What do I want?" to "What does God want?" As my pastor, Jonathan Pokluda, said, "Our earthly romantic relationships are supposed to be a reflection of, or a peek into, our eternal relationship with our Savior."[3] A verse I clung to in my single season of life was Matthew 6:33. It says, "Seek first the kingdom of God and his righteousness, and all these things will be added to you" (ESV). I coined a phrase that I'm sure has been used before: "Matthew 6:33 it." When you're anxious about getting married, feeling lonely, desiring to find contentment, or all these things, then "Matthew 6:33 it." Seek God and his will, and *everything* else will take care of itself. That's a guarantee.

As I end this chapter, I thought it would be fitting to include my vows to Madison Prewett Troutt. And as you read these, my prayer and hope is not that you would think, *I want a love like that.* But rather that you would see and be drawn to the incredible source of love we've built our relationship on. Because the love you are looking for is already yours: Jesus.

My Madi Rose,

I never knew a love could be so deep. I never knew God gave such beautiful and incredible gifts until he gave me you. I fell in love with you not because of your outward beauty but because of the beauty you carry inside. Who you are, alone with God, is the most beautiful thing about you.

Madi Rose Prewett, today I want to make my love and commitment permanent. I want you to know that by this ring I am committing to you for life. On your hard days, I choose you. On your sick days, I am with you. No matter the day, I will not go. I am completely and fully yours.

I do not complete you. I will fail you at times. I will not be enough at times. But I promise to always point you to the One that does complete you. His name is Jesus. I promise to lead you in humility, in honor and respect, as I follow God with my whole heart. I promise to be a man worth following. To be a man after God's own heart.

I promise to be gentle with you. To know where true strength comes from. To cherish your life above my own and be your greatest supporter and encourager. I promise to always pursue you and never stop dating you. I promise to fan the flame of your greatest strengths and to honor you always in public and in private. I promise to protect you. I promise to always cover you in prayer. To clothe you in God's Word.

Jesus says in John 15:13, "Greater love has no one than this, that someone lay down his life for his friends."[4] And you're my best friend in the whole world. I promise to consistently and constantly lay my life down for you. Always.

Through sickness and in health, for richer or poorer, I am yours and you are mine. My Madi.

# ACKNOWLEDGMENTS

Grant: You gave me and those around me hope that true love—God's best—is worth the wait and worth the fight. It hasn't always been easy. But thank you for always pointing me back to the one true and perfect love: Jesus. I love you and I choose you forever.

Mom: Thank you for showing me through your actions, prayers, and words what unconditional, sacrificial love looks like. You continuously laid down your life for Mallory, Mary, and me. You showed me how to be a woman of God and how to be a godly wife. I wouldn't be who I am and where I am without your love.

Dad: Thank you for loving Mom well and showing Mallory, Mary, and me from a young age what to look for in a godly man. Thank you for always believing in me. I wouldn't be who I am without your belief.

Mallory: Your loving heart is full of compassion and grace. You are faithful and loyal to those you love. The way you love others pleases the Lord and inspires me every day. You make everyone's life better, and it's truly beautiful.

Mary: Your loving heart is full of confidence and composure. Your love for Jesus is contagious. You are sure of what matters most, and your love is needed in this world.

Mrs. Lisa: You are a second mom to me. I have prayed for a mother-in-law like you, and you exceeded all expectations. Thank you for loving me like your own.

Mimi Delores: Thank you for demonstrating your love with a gentle and humble spirit and with passionate prayer. Your prayers over my mom and dad have created a ripple effect that has had a direct impact on my life and marriage and I know will have an impact on generations to come. Your prayers and love are felt by everyone around you.

Meme Glenda: Thank you for demonstrating your love with consistency and intentionality. You have shown me how to live an intentional life—a life on mission and on purpose. Your encouraging messages, letters, and meaningful gifts mean more than you will ever know.

Sydney: Your loving heart is full of kindness and service. Even amid trial and suffering, you find ways to serve and give—the true definition of a heart for Jesus. I wouldn't be where I am without you.

JP and Monica: Thank you for believing in me and Grant, leading with spirit, and being full of humility, wisdom, and authenticity. You both inspire us and set an incredible example of what a godly marriage and relationship looks like.

Jeanine: Your friendship has been a rock for me. As iron sharpens iron, you make me better and stronger. You have loved me through my highs and lows. And you helped prepare me to be a wife. I love you always.

Erica: You have been an inspiration to me since the moment I met you. And now I get to call you my best friend. God is just that good. You love with kindness and humility but also with passion, creativity, and care. I love you always, and my little Charlie Rose.

Jennie: Your love is strong. You give people the strength and hope to keep going. Your belief in me has meant more than you will ever know. You and Zac have helped Grant and me through all our relational twists and turns, highs and lows. We love y'all.

The Fedd Agency: Thank you for taking a chance on me and believing in me from the beginning. I am so grateful for your love, patience, and grace.

The WaterBrook team: Thank you for your belief in this message and in me. Thank you for being prayerful, intentional, and wise with this book—in making sure that every word was written with thought and belief. Y'all are the dream team and an answer to many prayers.

To all my other friends and family: Your love has carried me through and pushed me onward. Your prayers have held me up when I was weak, your encouragement has kept me going when I was doubtful, and your constant presence in my life has made me who I am today. I love you.

To you, my reader friends: You are so loved. When I felt like giving up on love in the past, I thought about you. When

I felt like giving up on this book, I thought about you—because you are worthy of the love you were created for. I pray that as you read this book, you felt challenged and encouraged, maybe even to raise your standards for relationships. But most importantly, I pray that you encounter the greatest love of all: Jesus.

# NOTES

## Chapter 2: He Loves Me, He Loves Me Not

1. Shania Twain, "Man! I Feel like a Woman!," *Come On Over*, Mercury Records, 1997.
2. Drake, "Fake Love," by Aubrey Graham et al., *More Life*, Cash Money Records, 2017.
3. Micah Berteau, *Love Changes Everything: Finding What's Real in a World Full of Fake* (Grand Rapids: Revell, 2019), 15.

## Chapter 3: Pick Me

1. Madison Prewett, *Made for This Moment: Standing Firm with Strength, Grace, and Courage* (Grand Rapids: Zondervan Books, 2021), 97–98.

## Chapter 4: If He Wanted to, He Would

1. Madison Prewett, *Made for This Moment: Standing Firm with Strength, Grace, and Courage* (Grand Rapids: Zondervan Books, 2021), 177–79.

## Chapter 6: Love Is Blind

1. Glenn Stanton, "Does Faith Reduce Divorce Risk?," Public Discourse, March 22, 2018, www.thepublicdiscourse.com/2018/03/20935.

## Chapter 7: In My Feelings

1. Andy Stanley, *The New Rules for Love, Sex, and Dating* (Grand Rapids: Zondervan, 2014), 24.
2. Gary Thomas, *The Sacred Search: What If It's Not About Who You Marry, but Why?*, rev. ed. (Colorado Springs: David C Cook, 2021), 26.
3. Rich Wilkerson, Jr., "Break Up or Break Down," Liberty University, www.liberty.edu/osd/lu-stages/2019/03/20/break-up-or-break-down-rich-wilkerson.

## Chapter 8: Shame on You

1. Lisa Bevere, Facebook, March 14, 2016, www.facebook.com/lisabevere.page/photos/a.284485715446/10156562418815447/?type=3.
2. Official Proverbs 31 Ministries, "Therapy and Theology: Good Guilt vs. Destructive Shame," video, 44:07, April 6, 2021, www.youtube.com/watch?v=rDpHf8LR8J0.
3. For a deeper understanding of shame, visit Brené Brown's website (https://brenebrown.com), watch her TED Talk on shame (www.ted.com/talks/brene_brown_listening_to_shame), or read her book *I Thought It Was Just Me (but It Isn't): Making the Journey from "What Will People Think?" to "I Am Enough"* (New York: Avery, 2007).
4. Brené Brown, "Listening to Shame," TED, March 2012, www.ted.com/talks/brene_brown_listening_to_shame.
5. Brené Brown, "Shame vs. Guilt," Brené Brown, January 15, 2013, https://brenebrown.com/articles/2013/01/15/shame-v-guilt.
6. Google Dictionary, s.v. "conviction."
7. Micah Berteau, *Love Changes Everything: Finding What's Real in a World Full of Fake* (Grand Rapids: Revell, 2019), 79–80.

## Chapter 9: thank u, next

1. Ariana Grande, "thank u, next," by Ariana Grande et al., *thank u, next*, Republic Records, 2019.

## Chapter 13: Season, Reason, or Lifetime?

1. Justin Bieber, "Lifetime," by Justin Bieber et al., *Justice (Triple Chucks Deluxe)*, Def Jam Recordings, 2021.

## Chapter 14: Marriage Material

1. John C. Maxwell, *Intentional Living: Choosing a Life That Matters* (New York: Center Street, 2015), 191.
2. Maxwell, *Intentional Living*, 193.

## Bonus Chapter: The Love He Wants

1. Kyle D. Killian, "Why Are Millennials the Loneliest Generation?," *Psychology Today*, March 22, 2024, www.psychologytoday.com/us/blog/intersections /202403/why-are-millennials-the-loneliest-generation.
2. Timothy Keller (@timkellernyc), X, February 4, 2017, https://twitter.com /timkellernyc/status/827962481461035008?lang=en.
3. Jonathan Pokluda, *Outdated: Find Love That Lasts When Dating Has Changed* (Grand Rapids, Mich.: Baker Books, 2021), 33.
4. John 15:13, ESV.

## ABOUT THE AUTHOR

Madison "Madi" Prewett Troutt is the bestselling author of *Made for This Moment* and a speaker, social media influencer, and TV personality. Her life mission is to share the name of Jesus and to help women discover who they were made to be and where to find the truest form of love.

Madi is also passionate about outreach programs and has partnered with Adullam House, Make It Matter, Autlive, and Auburn Dream Center.

She and her husband, Grant, are enjoying their early years of marriage and telling people about Jesus.

Madi would love to connect with you! Find her here:

Instagram/Twitter/TikTok: @madiprew
Website: www.madiprew.com

## ABOUT THE TYPE

This book was set in Baskerville, a typeface designed by John Baskerville (1706–75), an amateur printer and typefounder, and cut for him by John Handy in 1750. The type became popular again when the Lanston Monotype Corporation of London revived the classic roman face in 1923. The Mergenthaler Linotype Company in England and the United States cut a version of Baskerville in 1931, making it one of the most widely used typefaces today.